The Commonwealth
of Independent States
Economies

The Commonwealth of Independent States Economies

Perspectives and Challenges

Marcus Goncalves and Erika Cornelius Smith

BEP BUSINESS EXPERT PRESS

The Commonwealth of Independent States Economies: Perspectives and Challenges

Copyright © Business Expert Press, LLC, 2017.

First published in 2017 by
Business Expert Press, LLC
222 East 46th Street, New York, NY 10017
www.businessexpertpress.com

ISBN-13: 978-1-94709-822-0 (paperback)
ISBN-13: 978-1-94709-823-7 (e-book)

Business Expert Press Economics Collection

Collection ISSN: 2163-761X (print)
Collection ISSN: 2163-7628 (electronic)

Cover and interior design by Exeter Premedia Services Private Ltd., Chennai, India

First edition: 2017

10 9 8 7 6 5 4 3 2 1

Printed in the United States of America.

For my International Business students at Nichols College, for the
great discussions about regional markets and the global markets
as a whole, and for keeping me on my toes; for my beloved wife Carla,
always patient and caring with me during these intense projects;
for my son Samir, who brings me so much pride; and for my other
two children, Andrea and Joshua (in memory), also treasures
in my life, for which I count the days to be reunited with.
To God be the glory!

—Marcus Goncalves,
Spring 2017

For my Political Science students at Nichols College, who inspire me
with their humor and tenacity; for my muses, Sophie, and Phoebe, who
inspire me with their curiosity and moments of pure joy; and for my spouse,
Andrew, who inspires me with his generosity and an abundant supply of
strawberry licorice. For all of this and more, I am truly blessed.

—Erika Cornelius Smith
Spring 2017

Abstract

The year 2016 marks the 25th anniversary of the official inauguration of the Commonwealth of Independent States (CIS), a free association of sovereign states comprised of Russia and 11 other republics that were formerly part of the Soviet Union (The CIS—Belarus, Moldova, and Ukraine; the South Caucasus—Azerbaijan, Armenia, Georgia plus disconnected Abkhazia and South Ossetia; and Central Asia—Kazakhstan, Kyrgyzstan, Tajikistan, Turkmenistan, and Uzbekistan. Although this loose association of states may not exist as a fixed-entity on the globe, it is believed that this bloc of countries will continue to build upon the various separate regions in the former Soviet space in the coming decade.

Despite major differences country-to-country, groups within each state share many common economic, political, and cultural characteristics, which many hope will fade with the passing of those generations that remember the common state. In this context, the Russian Federation holds a unique position in the Euro-Pacific area. Separate, distinct, but still bordering these regions and related to all of them to differing degrees, in the 2010s Russia will step up efforts to become an independent center of gravity in Northern Eurasia. Leaning on its CIS allies and partners, Moscow is willing to fortify its stance vis-à-vis its geopolitical competitors—the European Union in the west, and China in the east.

Nevertheless, the combination of factors that determined the plunge in the economy of the CIS since the second quarter of 2015 persists today. These factors included the sharp fall in commodities prices, restrictions on access to international capital markets due to sanctions against Russia and a deceleration in China, which is the region's main trading partner. Although economic conditions in most of the CIS economies are challenging, differences in growth dynamics persist. Oil and gas exporting countries, namely Azerbaijan, Kazakhstan, Russia, and Turkmenistan, are seeing economic conditions deteriorating rapidly because of the sharp fall in energy prices. Meanwhile, most of the labor-exporting countries (Armenia, Kyrgyzstan, Moldova, and Tajikistan) are seeing the deterioration in growth rates, mainly due to strong production in the agricultural sector and, in some cases, increased activity in the extractive sector.

This book provides a regional analysis, as well as country scan, of the CIS regional block economies. We will examine their history since the breakup of the formal Soviet Union and the formation of the CIS bloc, including creation of regional agreements such as the CIS Free Trade Area and the Eurasian Economic Union, a single economic market which now represents more than 180 million people. As a whole, our text attempts to better understand current, and future, prospects for economic growth in the region, as well as their individual national challenges.

Keywords

CIS, Commonwealth of Independent States, EU, European Union, Eurozone, Russia Federation

Contents

Preface

This book is divided into six chapters, each addressing a significant aspect of the economic, political, and social transition in commonwealth of independent states (CIS) bloc over the last several decades. We integrate historical data with the most recent political and economic reporting in our analysis, including our assessments, opinions, and experience (where appropriate) as scholars, researchers, consultants, and global citizens.

Chapter 1 provides the reader with an introduction to the historical context for the CIS bloc, including the political structures and economic relationships forged in the post-World War II period. We pay close attention to the impact of nationalist histories and geography on the politics of integration, and include brief introductions to each country included in later chapters of this publication.

Chapter 2 provides an overview of the economic activity of the CIS region. We provide an overview of the geopolitical and economic challenges of the CIS bloc. We also discuss the economic challenges faced by these economies regionally, as well as in consequence of external forces brought by advanced economies, such as the global financial contagion resulted of the economic crisis that started in 2007, and the currency wars and their consequences to local and global economies.

Chapter 3 discusses the many challenges for foreign investors and multinational enterprises (MNEs) in entering the CIS economies, from skill mismatches and educational systems, to the impact of economic restructuring, legal framework, and trading policies. This chapter also provides an overview as to the main reasons why MNEs fail in the CIS markets.

Chapter 4 discusses the impact of the global economic crisis that started in 2007 on the CIS region, its challenges and implications as well as the perspectives for recovery.

Chapter 5 introduces multiple frameworks for the study of political risk in the CIS region, and provides an overview of this important field for the reader. The chapter proceeds with country-based case studies that include Freedom House scores and in-depth political analysis to assess the potential risk created by stable or reforming political institutions in each CIS state.

Chapter 6 provides future considerations and challenges faced by the CIS in its economic growth, taking into consideration the most recent reports as of spring of 2017.

An extensive, user-friendly appendix that provides additional country-specific case studies and analysis for the reader follows these chapters. Our hope is that this work will provide an introduction to the historical and political context of the culturally rich, vibrant, and rapidly changing region of the CIS. We have balanced this introduction with breadth and depth for the international business professional who desires to engage in the significant opportunities available to those willing to explore this very important region in transition.

Acknowledgments

There were many people who helped us during the process of writing this book. It would be impossible to keep track of them all. Therefore, to all that we have forgotten to list, please don't hold it against us!

We would like to thank Dr. Patrick Barron, professor at the Graduate School of Banking at the University of Wisconsin, Madison, and of Austrian economics at the University of Iowa, in Iowa City, for his contributions.

We also would like to thank Mr. Bo-Young Lin, from the Graduate Institute of International and Development Studies and United Nations Conference on Trade and Development (UNCTAD) for his support and insights. We would also like to express our appreciation to many corporate leaders who shared their views and experiences with us in the CIS region. Our special thanks go to the following leaders and great friends: Jörgen Eriksson, founding partner at Bearing Group Ltd, in London, United Kingdom; Ewelina Kroll, public relations manager at East Europe Consulting; Piotr Kozicki, business information security officer at Citigroup Global Fund Services in Warsaw, Poland; Julius Niedvaras, director of international business school at Vilnius University, Lithuania; Luc Jalllois Sr. vice president at LJL Consulting, Kiev, Ukraine; Galyna Konto, investment manager, Kiev, Ukraine; Markéta Remišovská, principal at Rizzo Associates, Praga, Czech Republic; and Dmitriy Lisenkov, hedge fund manager at The Russian Technology Fund, St. Petersburg, Russia.

We would also like to thank our International Business research assistant at Nichols College, Jeremy Berger, for his enthusiasm and dedication in supporting the completion of this project.

CHAPTER 1

An Overview of the Commonwealth of Independent States

Demokratizatsiya

The Commonwealth of Independent States (CIS), also known as the Russian Commonwealth, is a regional bloc of countries formed during the breakup of the Soviet Union, whose participating countries are some former Soviet Republics. The CIS is a loose association of countries. Although the CIS has few supranational powers, it is aimed at being more than a purely symbolic organization, nominally possessing coordinating powers in the realm of trade, finance, lawmaking, and security. It has also promoted cooperation on cross-border crime prevention.

The CIS was established on December 8, 1991, through the Belavezha Accords,[1] which also brought a legal end to the Soviet Union. A *New York Times* article published the next day observed:

> Ever since the August coup d'etat, the Soviet Union has been dying a lingering death, its final agony stretched over months of crisis and negotiations while it was kept alive by the frantic faith

---

[1] The Belavezha Accords is the agreement that declared the Soviet Union effectively dissolved and established the Commonwealth of Independent States (CIS) in its place. It was signed at the state dacha near Viskuli in Belovezhskaya Pushcha on December 8, 1991, by the leaders of three of the four republics-signatories of the Treaty on the Creation of the USSR, including the Russian President Boris Yeltsin, Ukrainian President Leonid Kravchuk, and Belarusian Parliament Chairman Stanislav Shushkevich.

of one man, Mikhail S. Gorbachev, the Soviet president…Today, the union died—if future historians will accept a death warrant signed by the patient itself as proof.[2]

The preamble of the Belavezha Accords stated that "the USSR as a subject of international law and a geopolitical reality no longer exists." Article 1 of the Accords read: "The High Contracting Parties shall constitute the Commonwealth of Independent States (CIS)." The agreement stated a desire to develop cooperation in political, economic, humanitarian, cultural, and other fields. Parties guaranteed their citizens equal rights and freedoms, irrespective of their nationality or other differences; accepted and respected the territorial integrity of each other and the inviolability of existing borders within the Commonwealth, as well as the openness of borders, free movement of citizens and transfer of information within the Commonwealth. Article 14 determined the city of Minsk the official seat of the coordinating bodies of the Commonwealth.

Leaders from Russia, Ukraine, and Belarus signed these accords, dissolving the 1922 Union Treaty.[3] Within 2 weeks, on December 21st, in the city of Alma-Ata (Kazakhstan), the heads of Armenia, Azerbaijan, Kazakhstan, Kyrgyzstan, Moldova, Tajikistan, Turkmenistan, and Uzbekistan, signed the Declaration on the establishment of the CIS, commonly referred to as the Alma-Ata Protocols.[4] These 11 countries were joined by Georgia in December 1993, bringing the total membership to 12 states (the Baltic Republics of Estonia, Lithuania, and Latvia never joined). Figure 1.1 illustrates the geographic location of the CIS bloc.

---

[2] http://nytimes.com/1991/12/09/world/the-union-is-buried-what-s-being-born.html

[3] The Accords and other signed documents were ratified by the Supreme Soviet of the RSFSR on December 12, 1991. At the same time Russia dissolved the Union Treaty of 1922.

[4] The Alma-Ata Protocols are the founding declarations and principles of the CIS.

Figure 1.1 The 12 CIS bloc countries

Source: interopp.org.

Institutional Integration

The CIS Agreements articulate several goals for the organization, including coordination of members' foreign and security policies, development of a common economic space (CES), fostering human rights and inter-ethnic concord, maintenance of the military assets of the former USSR, creation of shared transportation and communications networks, environmental security, regulation of migration policy, and efforts to combat organized crime. The CIS is composed of three categories of institutions through which it attempts to integrate states within the framework of the organization and accomplish these goals: Charter Bodies, Executive Bodies, and Bodies of Branch Cooperation.

The Charter Bodies of the CIS are: The Council of the Heads of States, the Council of the Heads of Governments, the Council of Foreign Ministers, the Council of Defense Ministers, the Council of Commanders-in-Chief of Frontier Troops, the Inter-Parliamentary Assembly, and the Economic Court.

The Executive Bodies of the CIS are: The Economic Council, the Council of Permanent Plenipotentiary Representatives of the States-Participants of the Commonwealth under Charter and Other Bodies of the Commonwealth, and the Executive Committee.

The Branches of Cooperation of the CIS are: Anti-Terrorist Center, Interstate Bank, Interstate Statistical Committee, Interstate Council on Standardization Metrology and Certification, Interstate Council on Emergency Situation of natural and Anthropogenic Character, Interstate Council on Antimonopoly Policy, Coordinating Council on the States-Participants on the CIS on Informatization under the regional Commonwealth in the Field of Communications, Electric Energy Council, Interstate Council on Aviation and Air Space Use, Council of the Heads of Statistical Services of the States-Participants of the Commonwealth, Council of the Heads of Customs Services of the States-Participants of the Commonwealth, and more.

Council of the Heads of States

This is a supreme body of the CIS which discusses and solves any principle questions of the Commonwealth connected with the common interests of the States-Participants.

Council of the Heads of Governments

This Council coordinates cooperation of the executive authorities of the States-Participants in economic, social, and other spheres of their common interests. Decisions of the Council of the Heads of States and the Council of the Heads of Governments are adopted by consensus. Any state may declare about its lack of interest in one or another question, the fact being not considered as an obstacle for adopting a decision.

Council of Foreign Ministers

The main executive body ensuring cooperation in the field of foreign policy activities of the States-Participants of the CIS on the matters of mutual interest, adopting decisions during the period between the meetings of the Council of the Heads of States, the Council of the Heads of Governments and by their orders.

Council of Defense Ministers

This is a body of the Council of the Heads of States responsible for military policy of the States-Participants of the CIS. Its working office is a staff which coordinates military cooperation of the CIS member states, prepares and holds meetings of the Council of Defense Ministers, organizes the activities of groups of military observers and collective forces for peace keeping in the CIS.

Council of Commanders-in-Chief of Frontier Troops

This is a body of the Council of the Heads of States responsible for guarding outer frontiers of the States-Participants and securing stable situation there. Its working office is a Coordinating Service of the Council which organizes preparation and holding of the meetings of this Council, implementation of the decisions adopted by it.

Inter-Parliamentary Assembly

The Assembly was established in March 1995 by the leaders of Supreme Soviets (parliaments) of the Commonwealth countries as a consultative institution to discuss problems of parliamentary cooperation and develop proposals by the parliaments of the CIS states. It consists of parliamentary delegations of the States-Participants of the CIS. The activities of the Assembly are carried out by the Assembly Council which comprises the leaders of the parliamentary delegations. The Assembly Secretariat, headed by Secretary-General, was created to ensure the work of the Inter-Parliamentary Assembly, its Council and commissions.

Economic Court

The Economic Court functions with the aim of ensuring the meeting of economic commitments in the framework of the CIS. Its terms of reference include settlement of interstate economic controversy arising in meeting economic commitments envisaged by Agreements and decisions of the Council of the Heads of States and the Council of the Heads of Governments of the CIS.

Economic Council

The main executive body which ensures implementation of the decisions of the Council of the Heads of States and the Council of the Heads of Governments of the CIS on realization of the Agreement for creation of free trade zone, Protocol to it, as well as for other matters of socio-economic cooperation. The Council adopts the decisions on the matters related to its competence and by the orders of the Council of the Heads of States and the Council of the Heads of Governments of the CIS. Economic Council consists of the Deputy Heads of Governments of States-Participants of the CIS.

Executive Committee

It is the unite permanently functioning executive, administrative, and coordinating body of the CIS, which organizes the activities of the Council of the Heads of States, Council of the Heads of Governments, Council of Foreign Ministers of States-Participants of the CIS, Economic Council, and other bodies of the Commonwealth, prepares proposals on extending economic cooperation in the framework of the CIS, creating and functioning free trade zone, ensuring favorable conditions for transition to higher stage of economic cooperation, developing CES in future, jointly with the States-Participants and the bodies of the Commonwealth develops proposals and draft documents aimed at the development of States-Participants of the CIS in political, economic, social, and other spheres.

Integration Without Unification

Although the CIS was designed in some ways to replicate the economic, political, and historical relationships of the Soviet Union, it was not and is not a separate state or country. Rather, the CIS is an international organization designed to promote cooperation among its members in a variety of fields. Its headquarter is in Minsk, Belarus. Over the years, its members have signed dozens of treaties and agreements, and some hoped that it would ultimately promote the dynamic development of ties among the newly independent post-Soviet states. By the late 1990s, however, the CIS lost most of its momentum and was victimized by internal rifts, becoming, per some observers, largely irrelevant and powerless.[5]

From its beginning, the CIS had two main purposes. The first was to promote what was called a "civilized divorce" among the former Soviet states. Many feared the breakup of the Soviet Union would lead to political and economic chaos, if not outright conflict over borders. The earliest agreements of the CIS, which provided for recognition of borders, protection of ethnic minorities, maintenance of a unified military command, economic cooperation, and periodic meetings of state leaders, arguably helped to maintain some semblance of order in the region, although one should note that the region did suffer some serious conflicts, of note, the war between Armenia and Azerbaijan, and the civil conflicts in Tajikistan, Moldova, and Georgia.

The second purpose of the CIS was to promote integration among the newly independent states. On this score, the CIS had not succeeded. The main reason is that while all parties had a common interest in peacefully dismantling the old order, there has been no consensus among these states as to what, if anything, should replace the Soviet state. Moreover, the need to develop national political and economic systems took precedence in many states, dampening enthusiasm for any project of reintegration. CIS members have also been free to sign or not sign agreements as they see fit, creating a hodgepodge of treaties and obligations among CIS states.

Cooperation in military matters fared little better. The 1992 Tashkent Treaty on Collective Security[6] was ratified by a mere six states. While CIS peacekeeping troops were deployed to Tajikistan and Abkhazia, a region

---

[5] Andrew, R. 2015. "Donbas: A new 'black hole' in Europe," EU Observer, https://euobserver.com/foreign/128618, last accessed in 11/12/2015.

[6] The Collective Security Treaty Organization, also known as the "Tashkent Pact" or "Tashkent Treaty," is an intergovernmental military alliance that was signed on May 15, 1992 by six post-Soviet states belonging to the Commonwealth of Independent States, including Russia, Armenia, Kazakhstan, Kyrgyzstan, Tajikistan, and Uzbekistan. Three other post-Soviet countries, including Azerbaijan, Belarus, and Georgia, also signed the treaty on the following year. Five years later, six of the nine, all but Azerbaijan, Georgia, and Uzbekistan, agreed to renew the treaty for 5 more years, and in 2002 those six agreed to create the Collective Security Treaty Organization as a military alliance.

of Georgia, critics viewed these efforts as Russian attempts to maintain a sphere of influence in these states. As a "Monroeski Doctrine[7]" took hold in Moscow, which asserted special rights for Russia on post-Soviet territory, and Russia used its control over energy pipelines to put pressure on other states, there was a backlash by several states against Russia, which weakened the CIS.

Since that time, it has undergone many changes in response to global shifts in economy, politics, security, and conflict. To promote further economic opportunity and integration, in October 2000 the heads of five countries (Belarus, Kazakhstan, Kyrgyzstan, Russia, Tajikistan) signed an Agreement on the creation of Eurasian Economic Community (EAEC or EurAsEC).[8] In September 2003 Belarus, Kazakhstan, Russia, and Ukraine signed an Agreement on Formation of CES.[9] As a result of political upheavals between the years of 2003 and 2005, three CIS member states experienced a change of government in a series of color revolutions: Eduard Shevardnadze was overthrown in Georgia, Viktor Yushchenko was elected in Ukraine, and, lastly, Askar Akayev was toppled in Kyrgyzstan.[10]

While these political and economic shifts have impacted integration efforts, the movement of states in and out of various CIS Agreements and institutions has also created discontinuity and disruption. In October 2005 Uzbekistan stated its intention to join the CIS organization, while in February 2006, Georgia officially withdrew from the Council of Defense Ministers: it so happened that Georgia was working to join NATO and

---

[7] The "Monroeski Doctrine" was a colloquial description of Boris Yeltsin's foreign policy strategy in the near abroad. Adapted from the United States' 19th-century Monroe Doctrine, which prohibited European colonization of the newly independent Latin American republics, the Monroeski Doctrine affirmed the Russian Federation's position as the dominant power in the entire former Soviet Union. Moscow often invoked the doctrine when it intervened in post-Soviet conflicts in the Newly Independent States of Eurasia, such as the Tajik Civil War and the separatist conflicts in Nagorno-Karabakh, Transnistria, Abkhazia, and South Ossetiya.

[8] At present Armenia, Moldova, and Ukraine have the status of the observer under EAEC. For more on the EAEC, see Chapter 3 in this text.

[9] For more on the CES, see Appendix A country scans.

[10] For more on political risk and regime change, see Chapter 6.

could not be part of two military structures simultaneously. However, Georgia remained a full member of the CIS but following the South Ossetian war in 2008, President Saakashvili announced during a public speech in the capital city Tbilisi that Georgia would leave the CIS and the Georgian Parliament voted unanimously (on August 14, 2008) to withdraw from the regional organization. On August 18, 2008 the Ministry of Foreign Affairs of Georgia sent a note to the CIS Executive Committee notifying it of the aforesaid resolutions of the Parliament of Georgia and Georgia's withdrawal from CIS. In accordance with the CIS Charter, Georgia's withdrawal came into effect 12 months later, on August 18, 2009. Yet earlier that year, in May 2009 six countries Armenia, Azerbaijan, Belarus, Georgia, Moldova, and Ukraine joined the Eastern Partnership, a project which was initiated by the European Union.

After September 11, 2001, the CIS created bodies to help combat terrorism, and some hoped that this might bring new life to the organization. But within a short time of those efforts, in March 2007, Igor Ivanov, the secretary of the Russian Security Council, expressed his doubts concerning the usefulness of CIS, and emphasizing that the Eurasian Economic Community became a more competent organization to unify the biggest countries of the CIS.

Brief State Introductions

Brief introductions with data and analyses from the *CIA World Factbook* are provided in the following for each state, while a more thorough country scanning of CIS member states is included in Appendix A.

Armenia

Seated in Southwestern Asia, between Turkey (to the west) and Azerbaijan, Armenia views itself as part of Europe. Geopolitically, it can be classified as falling within Europe, the Middle East, or both. The eastern area of Armenia was ceded by the Ottomans to Russia in 1828; this portion declared its independence in 1918, but was conquered by the Soviet Red Army in 1920. It has only two open trade borders—Iran and Georgia—because its borders with Azerbaijan and Turkey have been closed since

1991 and 1993, respectively, as a result of Armenia's ongoing conflict with Azerbaijan over the separatist Nagorno-Karabakh region. Armenia's geographic isolation, a narrow export base, and pervasive monopolies in important business sectors have made it particularly vulnerable to the sharp deterioration in the global economy and the economic downturn in Russia. In 2015, the state joined Russia, Belarus, and Kazakhstan as a member of the Eurasian Economic Union and approved a constitutional referendum that will change the government type to a parliamentary system, replacing the semipresidential system and becoming effective for the 2017 through 2018 electoral cycle.

Recovering commodity prices and Russian economic activity should lead to a robust acceleration in GDP growth this year in Armenia. We see the economy expanding 2.8 percent in 2017, which is down 0.1 percentage points from earlier forecasts, and 3.4 percent in 2018.

Azerbaijan

A nation with a majority-Turkic and majority-Shia Muslim population, Azerbaijan is situated in Southwestern Asia on the border of the Caspian Sea, between Iran and Russia, with a small European portion north of the Caucasus range. The state was briefly independent (1918–1920) following the collapse of the Russian Empire, but was subsequently incorporated into the Soviet Union for seven decades. Azerbaijan has made only limited progress on instituting market-based economic reforms. Corruption in the country is widespread, and the government, which eliminated presidential term limits in a 2009 referendum and approved extending presidential terms from 5 to 7 years in 2016, has been accused of authoritarianism.

Azerbaijan's GDP growth should accelerate moderately in 2017, as oil and gas prices recover. We expect GDP to grow 1 percent in 2017. For 2018, panelists see growth accelerating to 2 percent.

Belarus

Belarus is located on the edge of Eastern Europe, just east of Poland. After seven decades as a constituent republic of the USSR, Belarus attained its independence in 1991, but has retained closer political and economic ties to Russia than have any of the other former Soviet Republics. It is a presidential republic in name, although most scholars argue that it is, in reality, a dictatorship (see Chapter 6). Economic output, which had declined for several years following the collapse of the Soviet Union, revived in the mid-2000s due to the boom in oil prices. As part of the former Soviet Union, Belarus had a relatively well-developed, though aging industrial base; however, much of it is now outdated, energy inefficient, and dependent on subsidized Russian energy and preferential access to Russian markets.

Belarus GDP purchasing power parity (PPP) was last recorded at $16,621.03 in 2015, which is equivalent to 94 percent of the world's average. GDP per capita PPP in Belarus averaged $10,505.09 from 1990 until 2015, reaching an all-time high of $17,348.06 in 2014 and a record low of $5,275.43 in 1995.

Georgia

Situated in Southwestern Asia and bordering the Black Sea, between Turkey and Russia, Georgia views itself as part of Europe. Like Armenia, geopolitically, it can be classified as falling within Europe, the Middle East, or both. Georgia was absorbed into the Russian Empire in the 19th century. Independent for 3 years (1918–1921) following the Russian revolution, it was forcibly incorporated into the USSR in 1921 and regained its independence when the Soviet Union dissolved in 1991. Periodic flare-ups in tension and violence culminated in a 5-day conflict in August 2008 between Russia and Georgia, with Russia unilaterally recognizing the independence of Abkhazia and South Ossetia and stationing military forces remain in those regions. Georgia's economy sustained GDP growth of more than 10 percent in 2006 through 2007, based on strong inflows of foreign investment and robust government spending. However, GDP growth slowed following the 2008 conflict with Russia. Although Georgia completed its withdrawal from the CIS in 2009, it is an important state to evaluate in the context of the organization's attempts at political and economic integration.

Despite the severe damage the economy of Georgia suffered due to civil strife in the 1990s, the country has been able to recover significantly by 2000, with the help of the IMF and World Bank. Robust GDP growth has been achieved since then. GDP growth, spurred by gains in the industrial and service sectors, remaining in the 9 to 12 percent range in 2005 through 2007, but during 2006 and in 2008, the World Bank named Georgia the top reformer in the world.[11]

Kazakhstan

Kazakhstan is located within Central Asia, northwest of China, in an area that was conquered by Russia in the 18th century. It became a Soviet Republic in 1936, and policies implemented by the Soviet government reduced the number of ethnic Kazakhs in the 1930s and enabled non-ethnic Kazakhs to outnumber natives. Through the mid-2000s, however, a national program has repatriated about a million ethnic Kazakhs back to Kazakhstan. The state's economy is larger than those of all the other Central Asian states largely due to the country's vast natural resources. Kazakhstan, geographically the largest of the former Soviet Republics, excluding Russia, possesses substantial fossil fuel reserves and other minerals and metals, such as uranium, copper, and zinc. The economic downturn of its EEU partner, Russia, and the decline in global commodity prices have contributed to an economic slowdown in Kazakhstan, which is experiencing its slowest economic growth since the financial crises of 2008 through 2009.

Kazakhstan is an upper-middle-income country with per capita GDP adjusted for PPP, of nearly $22,469 thousand in 2013. Its per capita GDP grew in 2014 although real GDP dropped due to internal capacity constraints in the oil industry, less favorable terms of trade, and an economic slowdown in Russia. The contribution of net exports to GDP growth improved materially followed by a sharp devaluation of the Kazakhstan tenge in February 2014, leading to a strong drop in imports of goods that became more costly. As a result of the devaluation, domestic inflation, as measured by the consumer price index (CPI), increased from 4.8 percent

---

[11] World Bank. 2015. "Doing Business: Georgia is This Year's Top Reformer," http://worldbank.org/en/country/georgia/overview, last accessed on 01/28/2016.

year-on-year in December 2013 to 6.9 percent in August 2014, due to higher imported input prices.

Kyrgyzstan

Most of the territory of present-day Kyrgyzstan, situated in Central Asia just to the west of China and south of Kazakhstan, was formally annexed to the Russian Empire in 1876. It became a Soviet Republic in 1936 and achieved independence in 1991 when the USSR dissolved. Kyrgyzstan is a mountainous country with an economy dominated by minerals extraction, agriculture, and reliance on remittances from citizens working abroad. It faced slow growth in recent years as the global financial crisis and declining oil prices have damaged economies across Central Asia, although Kyrgyz leaders hope the country's August 2015 accession to the Eurasian Economic Union will bolster trade and investment.

After independence in 1992, the Kyrgyz Republic's economy and public services were hit hard by the break-up of the Soviet economic zone and the end of subsidies from Moscow. Thanks to the adoption of market-based economic reforms in the 1990s, the economy has nearly recovered to its preindependence level of output, but infrastructure and social services have suffered from low investment. With a per capita PPP GDP of $2,920.60 in 2011, the Kyrgyz Republic remains a low-income country. Moreover, the global economic crisis, the political unrest of April and June 2010 and food price increases in 2011 and 2012 have reversed earlier gains in poverty reduction with GDP dropping to $2,869.82. The absolute poverty rate increased from 33.7 percent in 2010 to 36.8 percent in 2011.

Moldova

Located in Eastern Europe, Moldova formed part of Romania during the interwar period and was incorporated into the Soviet Union at the close of World War II. Although the country has been independent from the USSR since 1991, Russian forces have remained on Moldovan territory east of the Nistru River supporting the breakaway region of Transnistria. Despite recent progress, Moldova remains one of the poorest countries in Europe. The government's stated goal of EU integration has resulted in some market-oriented progress but over the longer term, Moldova's economy remains vulnerable to corruption, political uncertainty, Russian political and economic pressure, and unresolved separatism in the Transnistria region.

Moldova's economic performance over the last few years, has been relatively strong, aided by improved fiscal, monetary, and exchange rate policy. Moldova experienced the highest cumulative per capita PPP GDP growth, relative to the precrisis year of 2007, in the region. However, growth has been volatile because of climatic and global economic conditions. The GDP per capita in Moldova was last recorded at $4,753.55 in 2014, when adjusted by PPP. The GDP per capita, in the country, when adjusted by PPP is equivalent to 27 percent of the world's average. GDP per capita PPP in Moldova averaged $3,476.80 from 1990 until 2014, reaching an all-time high of $6,416.46 in 1990 and a record low of $2,267.88 in 1999.

Russia

The expansive territory of Russia includes North Asia bordering the Arctic Ocean, extending all the way from Europe (the portion west of the Urals) to the North Pacific Ocean. Historically speaking, repeated defeats of the Russian army in World War I led to widespread rioting in the major cities of the Russian Empire and to the overthrow in 1917 of the tsarist imperial government. The communists under Vladimir Lenin seized power soon after and formed the USSR. After defeating Germany in World War II as part of an alliance with the United States (1939–1945), the USSR expanded its territory and influence in Eastern Europe and emerged as a global power. The Soviet economy and society stagnated, however, in the decades following Stalin's rule, until General Secretary Mikhail Gorbachev (1985–1991) introduced *glasnost* (openness) and *perestroika* (restructuring) in an attempt to modernize communism. Most scholars believe his initiatives inadvertently released forces that by December 1991 splintered the USSR into Russia and 14 other independent states. Following economic and political turmoil during President Boris Yeltsin's term (1991–1999), Russia shifted toward a centralized, semi-presidential authoritarian state under the leadership of President Vladimir Putin (2000–2008, 2012–present). Russia has undergone significant changes since the collapse of the Soviet Union, moving from a centrally planned economy toward a more market-based system. The state is engaged in several territorial disputes with countries such as Japan, Georgia, Finland, Estonia, Ukraine, and Kazakhstan, and has outstanding negotiations with the United States, Denmark, Greenland, Norway, Lithuania, and China.

The Russian economy ranks as the 10th largest by nominal GDP and 6th largest by PPP as of 2015.[12] Russia's extensive mineral and energy resources, the largest reserves in the world, have made it one of the largest producers of oil and natural gas globally.[13] The country is one of the five recognized nuclear weapons states and possesses the largest stockpile of weapons of mass destruction. Russia was the world's second biggest exporter of major arms in 2010 through 2014, according to Stockholm International Peace Research Institute (SIPRI) data.[14]

Tajikistan

Located in Central Asia, west of China and south of Kyrgyzstan, Tajikistan is a poor, mountainous country with an economy dominated by minerals extraction, metals processing, agriculture, and reliance on remittances from citizens working abroad. The Tajik people came under Russian rule in the 1860s and 1870s, but Russia's hold on Central Asia weakened following the Revolution of 1917. Bands of indigenous guerrillas (called "basmachi") fiercely contested Bolshevik control of the area, which was not fully reestablished until 1925. Tajikistan became independent in 1991 following the breakup of the Soviet Union, and experienced a civil war between regional factions from 1992 to 1997. The country

---

[12] IMF. 2015. "Report for Selected Countries and Subjects," http://imf.org/external/pubs/ft/weo/2015/01/weodata/index.aspx, last accessed on 01/28/2016.

[13] International Energy Agency. 2012. "Oil Market Report," https://web.archive.org/web/20120518015934/http://omrpublic.iea.org/omrarchive/18jan12sup.pdf, last accessed 01/28/2016.

[14] Stockholm International Peace Research Institute. 2014. "Trends in International Arms Transfer, 2014," http://books.sipri.org/product_info?c_product_id=495, last accessed 01/28/16.

remains the poorest in the former Soviet sphere. Although it became a member of the World Trade Organization in March 2013, its economy continues to face major challenges, including dependence on remittances from Tajikistanis working in Russia, pervasive corruption, and the opiate trade in neighboring Afghanistan.

Tajikistan's GDP per capita was last recorded at $2,532.51 in 2016, when adjusted by PPP. The GDP per capita, in Tajikistan, when adjusted by PPP is equivalent to 14 percent of the world's average. GDP per capita PPP in Tajikistan averaged $1,849.28 from 1990 until 2014, reaching an all-time high of $3,635.34 in 1990 and a record low of $1,040.23 in 1996.

Turkmenistan

Present-day Turkmenistan, situated in Central Asia and bordering the Caspian Sea, between Iran and Kazakhstan covers territory that has been at the crossroads of civilizations for centuries. The area was once ruled in antiquity by various Persian empires, and was conquered by Alexander the Great, Muslim armies, the Mongols, Turkic warriors, and eventually the Russians. Annexed by Russia in the late 1800s, Turkmenistan later figured prominently in the anti-Bolshevik movement in Central Asia. In 1924, Turkmenistan became a Soviet Republic; it achieved independence upon the dissolution of the USSR in 1991. Largely a desert country with intensive agriculture in irrigated oases and significant natural gas and oil resources, it is reported that 60 percent of gas exports are currently sent to China and the remainder to Russia and Iran.

The Turkmen economy continued strong growth performance in 2016, expanding by 11.1 percent. High growth performance sustained over an extended period of time led to a steady increase in income levels and moved the country to an upper-middle income status. Preliminary outcomes of the annual economic developments demonstrate that the Turkmen economy remains resilient to the global uncertainties stemming from the Eurozone crisis. The GDP per capita in Turkmenistan was last recorded at $14,762.19 in 2015, when adjusted by PPP. The GDP per capita, in Turkmenistan, when adjusted by PPP is equivalent to 83 percent of the world's average. GDP per capita PPP in Turkmenistan averaged $7,471.40 from 1990 until 2014, reaching an all-time high of $14,762.19 in 2014 and a record low of $4,221.14 in 1997.

Ukraine

Located on the east of Europe and bordering the Black Sea, between Poland, Romania, and Moldova in the west and Russia in the east, Ukraine was the center of the first eastern Slavic state, Kyivan Rus, which during the 10th and 11th centuries was the largest and most powerful state in Europe. Although Ukraine achieved a short-lived period of independence (1917–1920), it did not achieve final independence until 1991 with the dissolution of the USSR. After Russia, the Ukrainian Republic was the most important economic component of the former Soviet Union, producing about four times the output of the next-ranking republic. Yet, democracy and prosperity remain elusive as the legacy of state control and endemic corruption has stalled efforts at economic reform, privatization, and civil liberties. This is further complicated by regional security threats, including Russia's occupation of Crimea in March 2014 and ongoing aggression in eastern Ukraine–both of which have hurt economic growth. Russia also continues to supply separatists in two of Ukraine's eastern provinces with manpower, funding, and materiel resulting in an armed conflict with the Ukrainian Government. Representatives from Ukraine, Russia, and the Organization for Security and Cooperation in Europe meet regularly to facilitate implementation of a peace deal, but scattered fighting between Ukrainian and Russian-backed separatist forces is still ongoing in eastern Ukraine.

Ukraine's GDP per capita PPP was last recorded at $8,267.07 in 2016, when adjusted by PPP. The GDP per capita, in Ukraine, when adjusted by PPP is equivalent to 47 percent of the world's average. GDP per capita PPP in Ukraine averaged $6,996.86 from 1990 until 2014, reaching an all-time high of $10,490.37 in 1990 and a record low of $4,462.78 in 1998.

Uzbekistan

Russia conquered the territory of present-day Uzbekistan, located in Central Asia, north of Turkmenistan and south of Kazakhstan, in the late 19th century. Uzbekistan is a landlocked country with more than 60 percent of the population living in densely populated rural communities. Resistance to the Red Army after the Bolshevik Revolution was eventually suppressed and a socialist republic established in 1924. Since its independence in September 1991, the government maintained its Soviet-style command economy with subsidies and tight controls on production and prices. Uzbekistan's first president following independence, Islom Karimov, led Uzbekistan for 25 years until his death in August 2016. The political transition to his successor was peaceful, but did not follow constitutional processes that would have named the chairman of the Senate as acting president. Recently, lower global commodity prices and economic slowdown in neighboring Russia and China have been hurting Uzbekistan's trade and investment and worsening its problem of currency shortage.

Since the mid-2000s, Uzbekistan has enjoyed robust GDP growth, thanks to favorable trade terms for its key export commodities like copper, gold, natural gas, cotton, the government's macro-economic management, and limited exposure to international financial markets that protected it from the economic downturn. Still, the future is not without challenges. The GDP per capita in Uzbekistan was last recorded at $5,319.50 in 2014, when adjusted by PPP. The GDP per capita, in Uzbekistan, when adjusted by PPP is equivalent to 30 percent of the world's average. GDP per capita PPP in Uzbekistan averaged $3,164.74 from 1990 until 2014, reaching an all-time high of $5,319.50 in 2014 and a record low of $2,216.68 in 1996.

CHAPTER 2

Economic Activity in the CIS Region

Overview

One of the clearest failures of the CIS has been on the economic front. Although the member states pledged cooperation, things began to break down early on. By 1993, the ruble zone collapsed, with each state issuing its own currency. In 1993 and 1994, eleven CIS states ratified a Treaty on an Economic Union, in which Ukraine joined as an associate member. A free-trade zone was proposed in 1994, but by 2002 it still had not yet been fully established. In 1996 four states, including Russia, Belarus, Kyrgyzstan, and Kazakhstan, created a Customs Union,[1] but others refused to join. All these efforts were designed to increase trade, but, due to several factors, trade among CIS countries has lagged targeted figures. More broadly speaking, economic cooperation has suffered because states had adopted economic reforms and programs with little regard for the CIS and have put more emphasis on redirecting their trade to neighboring European or Asian states.

Economic Challenges

Per Marek Dabrowski,[2] a scholar and Professor at the Higher School of Economics in Moscow and Fellow at CASE—Centre for Social and Economic Research in Warsaw, the period of fast economic growth and

---

[1] A group of countries that have agreed to charge the same import duties as each other and usually to allow free trade between themselves.

[2] Dabrowski, M. 2015. "It is not just Russia: current crisis in the CIS." Bruegel Policy Contribution, Issue 2015/01, February 2015, http://bruegel.org/wp-content/uploads/imported/publications/pc_2015_01_CIS_.pdf, last accessed on 01/10/2016.

relative macroeconomic stability in the CIS seems to be over. The collapse of the Russian ruble, expected recession in Russia, the stronger U.S. dollar and lower commodity prices have negatively affected the entire region through trade, labor remittance, and financial-market channels, resulting in negative expectations and leading to either substantial depreciation of national currencies, or decline in countries international reserves, or both. This means that the EU's entire eastern neighborhood faces serious economic, social, and political challenges coming from weaker currencies, higher inflation, decreasing export revenues and labor remittances, net capital outflows and stagnating or declining GDP.

The currency crisis started in Russia and Ukraine during 2014 because of the combination of global, regional and country-specific factors. Among the latter, the ongoing conflicts between the two countries and the associated U.S. and EU sanctions against Russia have played the most prominent role. At the end of 2014 and in early 2015, the currency crisis spread to Russia and Ukraine's neighbors.

The gradual depreciation of the ruble against both the euro and U.S. dollar, as depicted in Figure 2.1, started in November 2015, before the Russian-Ukraine conflict emerged and when oil prices were high. The depreciation intensified in March and April 2014, after Russia's annexation of Crimea and the first round of U.S. and EU sanctions against Russia. Between May and July 2014, the ruble partly regained its previous value.

The depreciation trend, however, returned in the second half of July 2014. Its pace increased in October with a culmination in mid-December 2014, as also depicted in Figure 2.1. After a massive intervention on the foreign exchange market and the adoption by Russia of other anticrisis measures the situation stabilized for a while. However, depreciation started again in January 2015, boosted by Moody's and Standard & Poor's downgrading of Russia's credit rating, and the subsequent escalation of the Donbass[3] conflict in the Ukraine.

---

[3] The War in Donbass, also known as the War in Ukraine or the War in Eastern Ukraine, is an armed conflict in the Donbass region of Ukraine. From the beginning of March 2014, demonstrations by pro-Russian and anti-government groups took place in the Donetsk and Luhansk oblasts of Ukraine, together commonly called the "Donbass," in the aftermath of the 2014 Ukrainian revolution and the Euromaidan movement.

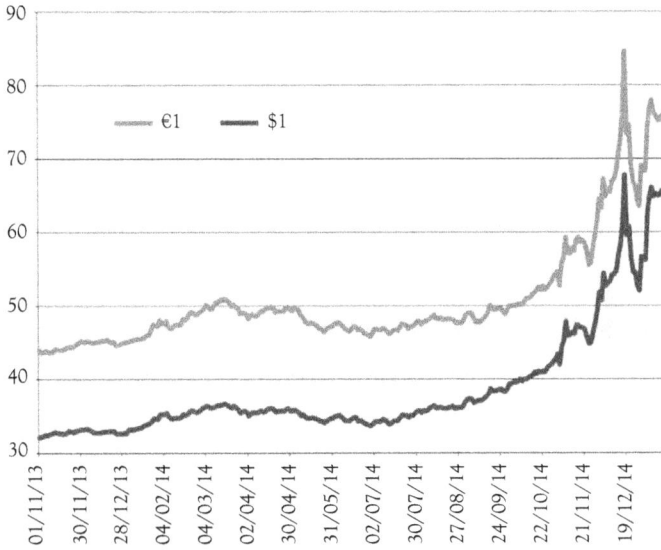

Figure 2.1 Ruble exchange rate against the euro and dollar, 2013–15

Source: Central Bank of Russia, http://cbr.ru/eng/currency_base/dynamics.aspx

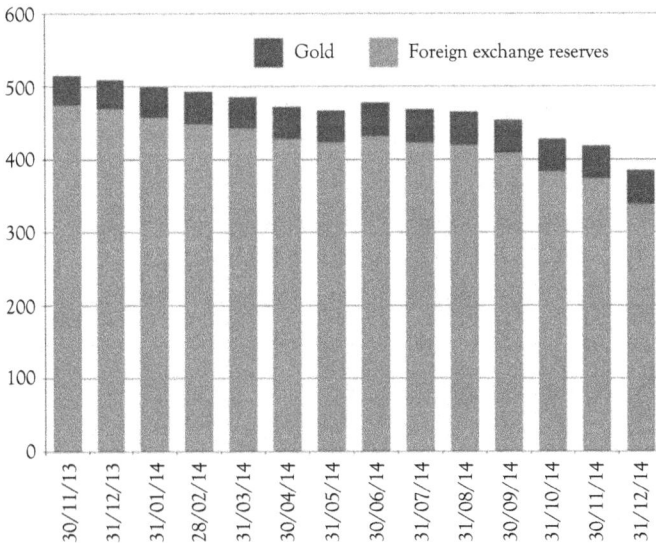

Figure 2.2 Russia's international reserves in $ billions, 2013–14

Source: Central Bank of Russia, http://cbr.ru/eng/hd_base/default.aspx?Prtid=mrrf_m

Cumulatively, between the end of November 2015 and end of 2014, Russia lost in the region $130 billion of its international reserves, as shown in Figure 2.2, which resulted from a large-scale capital outflow estimated to exceed $150 billion in 2014. Nevertheless, Russia continues to have a sizeable current account surplus. In the first half of January 2015, the reserves decreased further by about $7 billion.

Economies at War

This currency crisis challenges in Russia and in the CIS (more on this in the next section) is in fact a result of a much bigger threat to the global economy, often dubbed by economists at large because of currency wars. For the past few years, at least since 2010, government officials from the G7 economies have been very concerned with the potential escalation of a global economic war. Not a conventional war, with fighter jets, bullets, and bombs, but instead, a "currency war." Finance ministers and central bankers from advanced economies worry that their peers in the G20, which also include several emerging economies, may devalue their currencies to boost exports and grow their economies at their neighbors' expense.

Brazil led the charge, being the first emerging economy to accuse the United States of instigating a currency war in 2010, when the U.S. Federal Reserve bought piles of bonds with newly created money. From a Chinese perspective, with the world's largest holdings of U.S. dollar reserves, a U.S. lead currency war based on dollar debasement is an American act of default to its foreign creditors no matter how you disguise it. So far the Chinese have been more diplomatic, but their patience is wearing thin.

These two countries are not alone, as depicted in Figure 2.3, several other emerging markets, such as Saudi Arabia, Korea, Russia, Turkey and Taiwan have also been impacted by a weak dollar. That "quantitative easing" (QE) made investors flood emerging markets with hot money in search of better returns, which consequently lifted their exchange rates. But Brazil was not alone, as Japan's Shinzo Abe, the new prime minister, has also reacted to the QEs in the United States and pledged bold stimulus to restart growth and vanquish deflation in the country.

As advanced economies, like the first three largest world economies—United States, China, and Japan respectively—try to kick-start their sluggish economies with ultralow interest rates and sprees of money printing,

Exchange rates, rebased

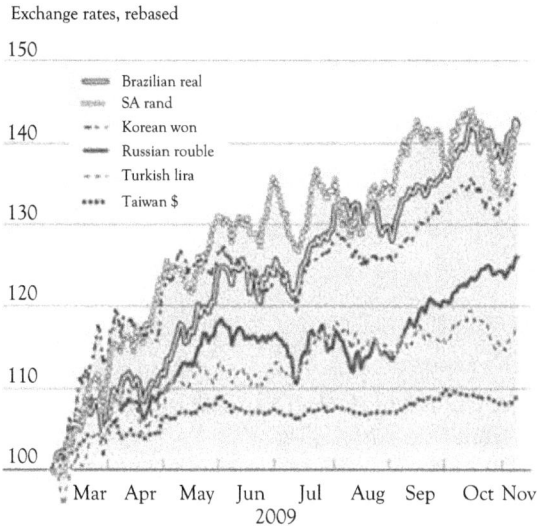

Figure 2.3 Emerging market currencies inflated by weak dollar

Source: Thompson Reuters Datastream.

they are putting downward pressure on their currencies. The loose monetary policies are primarily aimed at stimulating domestic demand. But their effects spill over into the currency world.

Japan is facing charges that it is trying first and foremost to lower the value of its currency, the yen, to stimulate its economy and get the edge over other countries. The new government is trying to get Japan, which has been in recession, moving again after a two-decade bout of stagnant growth and deflation. Hence, it has embarked on an economic course it hopes will finally jump-start the economy. The government pushed the Bank of Japan to accept a higher inflation target, which has triggered speculation the bank will create more money. The prospect of more yen in circulation has been the main reason behind the yen's recent falls to a 21-month low against the dollar and a near 3-year record against the euro.

Since Shinzo Abe called for a weaker yen to bolster exports the currency has fallen by 16 percent against the dollar and 19 percent against the euro. As the yen falls, its exports become cheaper, and those of Asian

How many yen one dollar buys

¥95 .... [Mon. Y92.376]

90 ....

85 .... Weaker ....

80 ....

75

70
2011 '12   '13

How many yen one euro buys

$1.50 ....

[Mon. $1.3514]

1.40 ....

1.30 ....

1.20 ....

1.10
2011 '12   '13

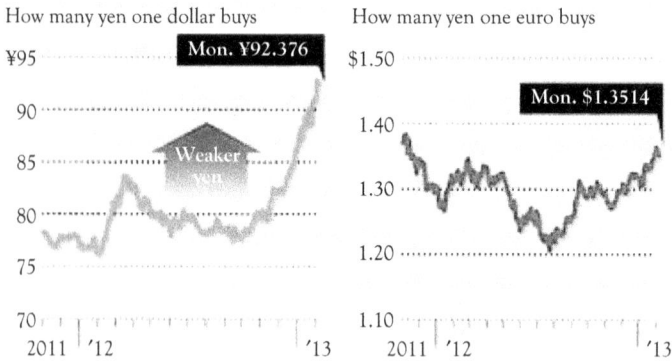

Figure 2.4 *Central banks in the United States and Japan have flooded their economies with liquidity*

Source: WSJ Market Data Group.

neighbors South Korea and Taiwan, as well as those countries further afield in Europe, become relatively more expensive. As depicted in Figure 2.4, central banks in the United States and Japan have flooded their economies with liquidity since mid-2012 into 2015, causing the yen and the dollar to weaken against other major currencies.

In our opinion, common sense could prevail, putting an end to the dangerous game of beggar (and blame) thy neighbor. After all, the International Monetary Fund was created to prevent such races to the bottom, and should try to broker a truce among foreign exchange competitors. The critical issues in the United States, as well as China and Japan, stem from minimally a blatantly ineffective public policy, but overridingly a failed and destructive economic policy. These policy errors are directly responsible for the opening salvos of the currency war clouds now looming overhead.[4]

---

[4] Our opinion expressed here is from the point of you of international trade and currency exchange as far as it affects international trade, and not from the geopolitical and economic aspects of the issue. We approach the issue of currency wars not from the theoretical, or even simulation models undertaken from behind a desk in an office, but from the point of view of practitioners engaged in international business and foreign trade, on the ground, in four different countries.

So far, Europe has felt the impact of the falling yen the most. At the height of the Eurozone's financial crisis in 2012, the euro was worth $1.21, which was potentially benefitting big exporters like BMW, AUDI, Mercedes, or Airbus. However, at the time of these writing, December 2015, the euro is at $1.38 even though the Eurozone is still the laggard of the world economy.

Across the 17-strong euro area a recovery has got under way following a double-dip recession lasting 18 months, but it is a feeble one. For 2015 GDP, will continue to fall by 0.4 percent (after declining by 0.6 percent in 2012), but it is expected to rise by 1.1 percent in 2014.[5] A rise in the value of euro, which is also partly to do with the diminishing threat of a collapse of the currency, will do little to help companies in the Eurozone—and will hardly help getting it growing again.

Chinese policy makers reject the conventional thinking proposed by advanced economies. How about the yen's extraordinary rise over the last 40 years, from JPY360 against the dollar at the beginning of the 1970s to about JPY102 today?[6] Not to mention that despite this huge appreciation, Japan's current account surplus has only got bigger, not smaller. They could also argue that the United States' prescription for China's economic rebalancing, a stronger currency and a boost to domestic demand, was precisely the policy followed by the Japanese in the late-1980s, leading to the biggest financial bubble in living memory and the 20-year hangover that followed.

Furthermore, the demand by the United States, which is backed by the G7 for a renminbi revaluation, is, in our view, a policy of the United States' default. During the Asian crisis in 1997 through 1998, advanced economies, under the auspices of the IMF, insisted that Asian nations, having borrowed so much, should now tighten their belts. Shouldn't advance economies be doing the same? In addition, Chinese manufacturing margins are so slim that significant change in exchange rates could wipe them out and force layoffs of millions of Chinese. As it is, labor

---

[5] The Economist's Writers 2015. "Taking Europe's pulse." *The Economist*, 11/05/2015. http://economist.com/blogs/graphicdetail/2015/11/european-economy-guide. Last accessed on 12/13/2015.
[6] As of December 2015.

rates are already climbing in China, further squeezing margins. Lastly, a revaluation of the yuan would only push manufacturing to other cheaper emerging markets, such as Vietnam, Cambodia, Thailand, Bangladesh, and other lower-paying nations without improving the advanced economies trade deficits.

Notwithstanding, some G7 policy makers believe these grumbles are overdone; arguing that the rest of the world should praise the United States and Japan for such monetary policies, suggesting the Eurozone should do the same. The war rhetoric implies that the United States and Japan are directly suppressing their currencies to boost exports and suppress imports, which in our view is a zero-sum game, which could degenerate into protectionism and a collapse in trade.

These countries, however, do not believe such currency devaluation strategy will threaten trade. Instead, their belief seems to be that as central banks continue to lower their short-term interest rate to near zero, exhausting their conventional monetary methods, they must employ unconventional methods, such as QE, or trying to convince consumers that inflation will raise. Their goal with these actions is to lower real (inflation-adjusted) interest rates. If so, inflation should be rising in Japan and in the United States, which as per Figure 2.5 it is.

As Figure 2.5 also shows, over the past decade, Japan has seen the consumer price index (CPI) for most periods hover just below the

JAPAN INFLATION RATE
Annual change on consumer price index

Figure 2.5 Japan's inflation rate has been climbing since 2010 because of economic stimulus

Source: Trading Economics,[7] Japan's Ministry of Internal Affairs and Communications.

---

[7] http://tradingeconomics.com, last accessed on 09/12/2015.

zero-percent inflation line. The notable exceptions were in 2008, when inflation rose as high as 2 percent, and in late 2009, when prices fell at close to a 2 percent rate. The rise in inflation coincided with a crash in capital spending. The worst period of deflation preceded an upturn. Of course, the earlier figure does not provide enough data to infer causal effects, but it seems, however, that the relationship between growth and Japan's mild deflation may be more complicated than the Great Depression-inspired deflationary spiral narrative suggests. The principal goal of this policy was to stimulate domestic spending and investment, but lower real rates usually weaken the currency as well, and that in turn tends to depress imports. Nevertheless, if the policy is successful in reviving domestic demand, it will eventually lead to higher imports.

At least that's how the argument goes. The IMF concluded that the United States' first rounds of QE boosted its trading partners' output by as much as 0.3 percent. The dollar did weaken, but that became a motivation for Japan's stepped-up assault on deflation. The combined monetary boost on opposite sides of the Pacific has been a powerful elixir for global investor confidence, if anything, to move hot money onto emerging markets where the interests were much higher than at advanced economies.

The reality is that most advanced economies have overconsumed in recent years. It has too many debts. But rather than dealing with those debts—living a life of austerity, accepting a period of relative stagnation—these economies want to shift the burden of adjustment on to its creditors, even when those creditors are relatively poor nations with low per capita incomes. This is true not only for Chinese but also for many other countries in Asia and in other parts of the emerging world. During the Asian crisis in 1997 through 1998, Western nations, under the auspices of the IMF, insisted that Asian nations, having borrowed too much, should now tighten their belts. But the United States doesn't seem to think it should abide by the same rules. Far better to use the exchange rate to pass the burden on to someone else than to swallow the bitter pill of austerity.

Meanwhile, European policy makers, fearful that their countries' exports are caught in this currency war crossfire, have entertained unwise ideas such as directly managing the value of the euro. While the option of generating money out of thin air may not be available to emerging markets, where inflation tends to remain a problem, limited capital

FTSE All-World indices,
rebased in $ terms

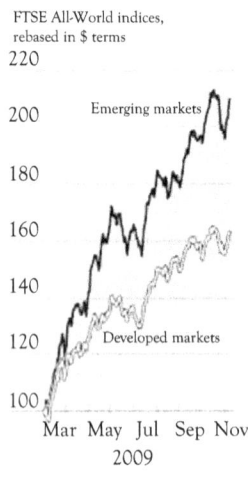

Figure 2.6 In 2009 emerging markets significantly outperformed advanced (developed) economies

Source: FTSE All-World Indices.

controls may be a sensible short-term defense against destabilizing inflows of hot money. Figure 2.6 illustrates how the inflows of hot money leaving advanced economies in search of better returns on investments in emerging markets have caused these markets to significantly outperform advanced (developed) markets.

Currency War May Cause Damage to Global Economy

As more countries try to weaken their currencies for economic gain, there may come a point where the fragile global economic recovery could be derailed and the international financial system thrown into chaos. That's why financial representatives from the world's leading 20 industrial and developing nations, spent most of their time during the G20 summit in Moscow in September 2015.

In September 2011, Switzerland acted to arrest the rise of its currency, the Swiss franc, when investors, looking for somewhere safe to store their cash from the debt crisis afflicting the 17-country Eurozone, saw in the Swiss franc the traditional instrument to fulfill that role. The Swiss intervention was viewed as an attempt to protect the country's exporters.

In our view, policy makers are focusing on the wrong issue. Rather than focus on currency manipulation, all sides would be better served to zero in on structural reforms. The effects of that would be far more beneficial in the long run than unilateral United States, China, or Japan currency action, and more sustainable. The G20 should focus on a comprehensive package centered on structural reforms in all countries, both advanced economies and emerging markets. Exchange rates should be an important part of that package, no doubt. For instance, to reduce the U.S. current-account deficits, Americans must save more. To continue to simply devalue the dollar will not be sufficient for that purpose. Likewise, China's current-account surpluses were caused by a broad set of domestic economic distortions, from state-allocated credit to artificially low interest rates. Correcting China's external imbalances requires eliminating these distortions as well.

As long as policy makers continue to focus on currency exchange issues, the volatility in the currency markets will continue to escalate. It has become so worrisome that the G7 advanced economies have warned that volatile movements in exchange rates could adversely hit the global economy. Figure 2.7 provides a broad view (rebased at 100 percent on August 1, 2008) of main exchange rates against the dollar.

When it became clear that Shinzo Abe and his agenda of growth-at-all-costs would win Japan's elections, the yen lost more than 10 percent

Figure 2.7 Exchange rates against the dollar

Source: Bloomberg.

against the dollar and some 15 percent against the euro. In turn, the dollar has also plumbed to its lowest level against the euro in nearly 15 months. These monetary debasement strategies are adversely impacting and angering export-driven countries such as Brazil, and many of the BRICS, ASEAN, CIVETS, and MENA blocs. But they also are stirring the pot in Europe. The Eurozone has largely sat out this round of monetary stimulus and now finds itself in the invidious position of having a contracting economy and a rising currency.

These currency moves have shocked BRICS countries as well as other emerging-market economies, including Thailand. The G20 is clearly divided between the advanced economies—the United Kingdom, the United States, Japan, France, Canada, Italy, Germany—and emerging countries such as Russia, China, South Korea, India, Brazil, Argentina, Indonesia, and the like. Top leaders of Russia, South Korea, Germany, Brazil, and China have all expressed their concern over the currency moves, which drive up the value of their currencies and undermine the competitiveness of their exports. If they decide to enter the game, like Venezuela, which has devalued its currency by 32 percent, the world would be plunged into competitive devaluations. At the end of the day, competitive devaluations would lead to run-away inflation or hyperinflation. Nobody will win with these currency wars.

James Rickards, author of "Currency Wars: The Making of the Next Global Crisis," expect the international monetary system to destabilize and collapse. In his views, "there will be so much money-printing by so many central banks that people's confidence in paper money will wane, and inflation will rise sharply.[8]"

If policy makers truly want to stage off this currency war, then it is a matter of doing what it was done in 1985 with the Plaza Accord.[9] This time, however, we will need a different version, as it will not be about the

---

[8] Francesco, G. 2015. "Currency War Has Started." *The Wall Street journal*, 02/04/2015. http://online.wsj.com/news/articles/SB10001424127887324761004578283684195892250. Last accessed on 12/13/2015.

[9] The Plaza Accord was an agreement between the governments of France, West Germany, Japan, the United States, and the United Kingdom, to depreciate the U.S. dollar in relation to the Japanese yen and German Deutsche Mark by intervening in currency markets. The five governments signed the accord on September 22, 1985 at the Plaza Hotel in New York City.

United States and the G5 of the time, in 1985. It must be an *Asian Plaza Accord* under the support and auspices of the G20. It must be about the Asia export led and mercantilist leadership agreeing amongst them. The chances of this happening, of advanced economies seeing the requirement for it, or these economies relinquishing its powers in any measurable fashion are not at all possible under the current political gamesmanship presently being played.

Currency War Also Means Currency Suicide

—Special contribution by Patrick Barron[10]

What the media calls a "currency war," whereby nations engage in competitive currency devaluations to increase exports, is really "currency suicide." National governments persist in the fallacious belief that weakening one's own currency will improve domestically produced products' competitiveness in world markets and lead to an export driven recovery. As it intervenes to give more of its own currency in exchange for the currency of foreign buyers, a country expects that its export industries will benefit with increased sales, which will stimulate the rest of the economy. So, we often read that a country is trying to "export its way to prosperity."

Mainstream economists everywhere believe that this tactic also exports unemployment to its trading partners by showering them with cheap goods and destroying domestic production and jobs. Therefore, they call for their own countries to engage in reciprocal measures. Recently Martin Wolfe in the Financial Times of London and Paul Krugman of *The New York Times* both accuse their countries' trading partners of engaging in this "beggar-thy-neighbor" policy and recommend that England and the United States respectively enter this so-called "currency war" with full monetary ammunition to further weaken the pound and the dollar.

I, Patrick, am struck by the similarity of this currency-war argument in favor of monetary inflation to that of the need for reciprocal trade

---

[10] Patrick Barron is a private consultant in the banking industry. He teaches in the Graduate School of Banking at the University of Wisconsin, Madison, and teaches Austrian economics at the University of Iowa, in Iowa City, where he lives with his wife of 40 years. We recommend you to visit his blog at http://patrick-barron.blogspot.com/ or contact him at PatrickBarron@msn.com.

agreements. This argument supposes that trade barriers against foreign goods are a boon to a country's domestic manufacturers at the expense of foreign manufacturers.

Therefore, reciprocal trade barrier reductions need to be negotiated, otherwise the country that refuses to lower them will benefit. It will increase exports to countries that do lower their trade barriers without accepting an increase in imports that could threaten domestic industries and jobs. This fallacious mercantilist theory never dies because there are always industries and workers who seek special favors from government at the expense of the rest of society. Economists call this "rent seeking."

Contagion Effect: The Spreading of the Crisis to CIS Member Countries

Since November 2014, the crisis has spread to number of former Soviet Union countries, especially Belarus, Armenia, Kyrgyzstan, and Moldova. It also affected, to a lesser extent, some countries in central and the CIS. The crisis-contagion mechanisms worked through several channels: Decreasing trade and deteriorating terms of trade with Russia, decreasing remittances from migrants working in Russia and, most importantly, the devaluation expectations of households and financial market players. Those former Soviet Union countries, for which Russia is an important trade partner, could not sustain continuation of the nominal appreciation of their currencies in relation to the ruble.

In addition, during the December 2014 phase of the CIS currency crisis a degree of contagion effect was visible on foreign exchange markets in central Europe, where currencies with flexible exchange rates depreciated against both the dollar and the euro. This affected the Hungarian forint, Serbian dinar, Polish zloty, Romanian leu, and Turkish lira. However, because of the limited trade and financial links between these countries and Russia and Ukraine, investors' negative reactions to these currencies were rather short-lived.

As discussed in the previous section, among the global factors that contributed to the CIS currency crisis, U.S. monetary policy seems to have played an important role. Since mid-2015, the expectation of the phasing down of QE 3, which eventually happened in October 2014, and more recently, expectations of an increase in the U.S. Federal Fund Rate

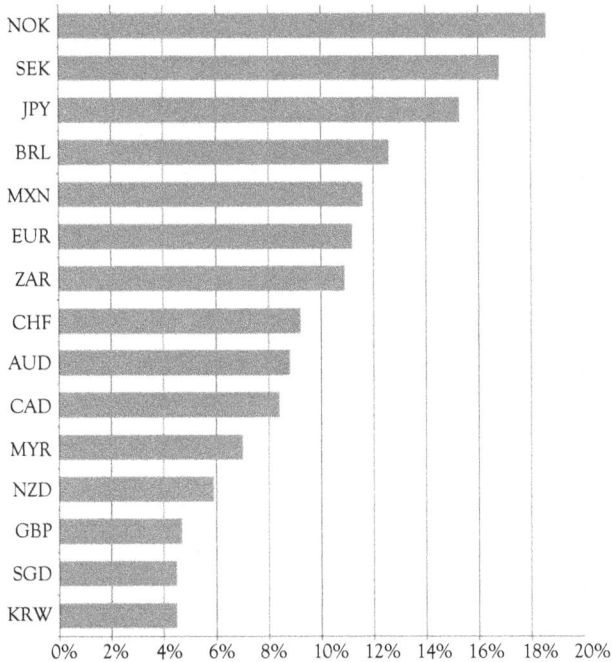

Figure 2.8 Depreciation against the dollar, in percent, December 2015 to December 2014, selected currencies

Source: U.S. Federal Reserve Board, http://federalreserve.gov/releases/g5/current/default.htm

in 2015,[11] has led to tighter global liquidity conditions. This could not be fully compensated for by simultaneous monetary policy easing in the euro area and Japan because of the much smaller size of financial markets in euro and yen. As result, net capital inflows into emerging-market economies decreased, growth in the latter decelerated and commodity prices started to fall[12] (see Feldstein, 2014 and Frankel 2015, on the effects of U.S. monetary tightening on oil and commodity prices). During 2014, as depicted in Figure 2.8, especially in the fourth quarter, the dollar appreciated against most currencies with flexible exchange rates.

---

[11] Darvas, Z. 2014. "Central Bank Rates Deep in Shadow." Bruegel blog, http://bruegel.org/nc/blog/detail/article/1497-central-bank-rates-deep-in-shadow/

[12] Feldstein, M. 2014. "The Geopolitical Impact of Cheap Oil." Project Syndicate, 26 November, http://project-syndicate.org/commentary/oil-prices-geopolitical-stability-by-martin-feldstein- 2014-11; Frankel, J. 2014. "The Euro Crisis: Where to From Here?," Faculty Research Working Paper Series, Harvard Kennedy School, RWP15-015.

CHAPTER 3

Challenges for Entering CIS Markets

Overview

As the advanced Western economies still try to recover fully from the global financial crisis, the CIS, a part of the world often neglected by investors and business leaders, has been showing impressive growth and maturity, both economically and politically. The International Monetary Fund (IMF) in its World Economic Outlook (2017) has improved the forecast for economic growth in the CIS countries up to 0.6 percent and 1.5 percent, in 2016 and 2017, respectively. IMF analysts also argue that many commodity exporters within the CIS still confront the need for sizable fiscal adjustments, and that these economies more broadly need to be alert to financial stability risks. Risks of noneconomic origin also remain salient, as political divisions within advanced economies, particularly between the United States and Russia at the starting of a new administration in the United States, may hamper efforts to tackle long-standing structural challenges and the refugee problem; and a shift toward protectionist policies is a distinct threat.

Recent political unrest in some countries of the region, however, threatens to stymie economic progress and has reminded investors of the inherent risk that such high-return opportunities tend to carry, along with other factors discussed in this chapter, which should be seriously considered.

Even when bound by the ideology and strong embrace of the Soviet Union, the CIS's countries differ widely, both economically and culturally. Hence, the CIS region has provided several new developments in information controls. The region witnessed two cyberwars. The first was a campaign by pro-Russian (and allegedly state-sponsored) hackers, which paralyzed the Estonian Internet in May 2007. The second was a similar campaign (also allegedly organized by nationalist pro-government Russian hackers) that occurred at the same time as major combat operations in Georgia (August 2008). The latter campaign targeting Georgian online media and government websites led Georgian authorities to filter access to Russian Internet sites (allegedly as a means of self-defense against Russian cyber propaganda) and resulted in an information vacuum in Tbilisi during the critical days where it was unclear whether Russian troops would stop their advance into Georgia.

Another important factor is the historical and cultural perspective that each country and its people possess. An investor would be well advised to seek trusted, and if possible local, advisers with a keen understanding of each country's culture and history. Failure to grasp local customs can be a pitfall when investing in any part of the world, but one would be hard pressed to find a place where such knowledge is more important than the CIS.

What helps promote international cooperation, particularly at a regional level? There is, of course, a broad literature on this topic, some of which is reviewed in more details throughout the book. Explanations tend to fall into four different categories: the importance of the structure of the international system; instrumental approaches often rooted in interdependence; state-level factors; and cultural-constructivist perspectives that emphasize development not so much of formal institutions but of a sense of region and regional identity.[1]

On the political side, newly elevated activists supported by democracy-hungry populations, along with some freshly repainted old-regime politicians, dominated the initial scrambles for power in these countries. After the early victories by the new but inexperienced leaders, however,

---

[1] This classification borrows much from Hurrell, A. 1995. "Regionalism in Theoretical Perspective," In *Regionalism in World Politics,* eds. L. Fawcett and A. Hurrell, 37–73. Oxford: Oxford University Press. Good sources that discuss regional theory and have relevance to the post-Soviet space are Kubicek, P. 1997. "Regionalism, Nationalism, and Realpolitik in Central Asia." *Europe-Asia Studies* 49, no. 4, pp. 637–55, and Bohr, A. 2004. "Regionalism in Central Asia: New Geopolitics, Old Regional Order." *International Affairs* 80, no. 3, pp. 485–502.

the former communist figures, well-groomed for political survival through the decades, have emerged as major players in many of these countries.

In addition, the global financial crisis that started in 2007 continues to ripple through these countries, and their ongoing struggle to adapt to new ways of doing business still bears watching, as does the potential for renewed political turmoil. In our experience teaching this topic, consulting for several multinational corporations around the world, and being a practitioner ourselves, we find that the CIS markets are not easy to enter. Hence, entering these markets can be a complex endeavor, but the rewards can be immense as well.

In some countries, government interference, backward infrastructure, political instability, works' skill mismatch, and even lack of skilled workers, requires a lot of patience, perseverance, and specialized assistance. Opportunities in the CIS markets, therefore, come with their own set of challenges.

Geopolitical Factors

Emerging economies, in particular the CIS economies have also experienced large-scale structural change. Neo-realism emphasizes international structure—commonly defined by the number of great powers in the global or, in this case, regional system—as crucial to explain both conflict and cooperation. Neo-realists tend to view regionalism as akin to alliance formation. One basic idea is that of balance of power—that states will form alliances and cooperative arrangements if they perceive some sort of threat. This threat can be from outside the region, so states may create regional arrangements to augment their own power. Examples would include the Gulf Cooperation Council (against Iran), ASEAN (against Vietnam), and MERCOSUR (against the United States). The threat, however, may also come from within the region itself, meaning that states might try to use multilateral institutions or regional integration to lock a regionally powerful state into a structure that can contain it. Arguably, the European Union (EU) has done so with respect to Germany,[2] and

---

[2] Grieco, J. 1995. "The Maastricht Treaty, Economic and Monetary Union, and the Neo-Realist Research Programme." *Review of International Studies* 21, no. 1, pp. 21–40.

this notion could be of great utility in the CIS, over which Russia casts a long shadow.

In contrast to the idea of balancing or being entrapped within regional institutions, some would emphasize the role of global or regional powers or hegemons in fostering cooperation. In addition to possessing resources that might overcome collective action problems, regional hegemons may see the growth of regional institutions, which they would dominate, as a means for furthering their own agenda, either within the region itself or with respect to the broader world. Other states would then bandwagon with the hegemon in the hope of receiving some benefits from the more powerful state or from regional structures themselves. The United States, for example, has helped foster many regional organizations, including NAFTA, the EU, the Gulf Cooperation Council, and ASEAN, all of which serve(d) both American and local interests.[3] The key, however, is that the willingness of other states to go along with the hegemon will be conditioned upon this commonality of interest. With respect to the CIS, the obvious hegemonic power is Russia. Thus, to the extent that Russia sees regionalism to its own advantage and other states see some benefit to attracting themselves to Russia, one might imagine that Russian-led regionalism would develop.[4]

When Vladimir Putin became President of Russia in 2000, he fully recognized Russia's diminishing role, both on the global stage and in the post-Soviet space. He pledged that relations with CIS states would be the high priority and took several steps to bolster Russia's role in the region. In the energy sphere, Putin pushed for more Russian investment in Caspian littoral states. He reached agreements with both Kazakhstan and Azerbaijan in 2001 to 2002 to resolve the legal status of drilling

---

[3] For the idea that regionalism could be an instrument for hegemonic control, see Mittelman, J., and R. Falk. 1999. "Hegemony: the Relevance of Regionalism?," In *National Perspectives on New Regionalism in the North,* eds. B. Hettne et al. London: Macmillan. See also Payne, A., and A. Gamble (eds). 1996. *Regionalism and World Order.* Basingstoke: MacMillan.

[4] For assessment of Russia's role as a hegemon with respect to Central Asia, see Allison, R. 2004. "Regionalism, Regional Structures Ad Security Management in Central Asia." *International Affairs* 80, no. 3, pp. 467–9.

rights in the Caspian. Putin also proposed increasing oil and gas ship-ments from the region through Russian pipelines to prevent construc-tion of alternative pipelines. This bore fruit, particularly with respect to Kazakhstan, which helped undercut Western efforts to get Kazakh oil to hook up to the BTC and flow westward. The planned export of Kazakh oil through Russian pipelines may, in the words of one report, give Rus-sia an "unbreakable stranglehold over Central Asia's energy reserves" and spell the end of United States and European-backed plans to build a trans-Caspian oil pipeline.[5] In addition, Russian concluded long-term contracts for the purchase of Turkmen gas, agreed in 2007 to upgrade gas pipelines flowing from Turkmenistan northward through Kazakhstan and Russia, and stepped up investments in energy fields in Uzbekistan.

In the security area, Russia has recovered from some of the setbacks it suffered after the United States stepped up its involvement after 9/11. It has maintained many of its bases in Central Asia whereas the Americans were kicked out of Uzbekistan in 2006 and have an uncertain future with basing rights in Kyrgyzstan. In 2002, six states—Russia, Belarus, Armenia, Kyrgyzstan, Tajikistan, and Kazakhstan—formed the Collective Security Treaty Organization (CSTO), an outgrowth of the 1992 CIS Collective Security Treaty. Uzbekistan joined in 2006. The CSTO has conducted joint military exercises and cooperates with the SCO, which has been increasingly visible in Central Asia and is viewed by both Russian and Chinese elites as a vehicle to balance American intrusions into both major powers' backyard. In 2003, for example, SCO members agreed to conduct military exercises and to set up a Secretariat for the organization in Beijing and an anti-terrorism center in Bishkek, Kyrgyzstan.

On economic questions, the EAEC has become the preeminent regional organization on the post-Soviet space. That may not be saying much, as many of its goals are more declaratory than implemented. What is interesting, however, is that much of its stated agenda is similar to orig-inal goals of the CIS, including creation of a customs union, general rules on trade in goods and services, a unified energy market, standardized cur-rency regulation, joint programs of social and economic development,

---

[5] 'Russia Celebrates Its Central Asian Energy Coup', Eurasianet.org, 16 May 2007.

harmonization of national legislation, and rights of individuals to obtain services for example educational, medical) in any state. Like the CIS, it has its own Secretariat, Inter-State Parliamentary Assembly, and State Councils. The Chinese, driven both by export markets and the need to diversify their energy supply, are also eager to give more of an economic component to the SCO.

If one counts all the aforementioned as evidence of successful regionalism, it is notable that none of this includes the CIS in its entirety. Regional integration has gone furthest between Russia and Belarus—which have flirted with the idea of unifying—and between Russia and Central Asian states. The latter is hardly surprising, rooted both in economic and security interdependence and common concerns about the West's democratization agenda, which included support for the 2003 Rose Revolution in Georgia, the 2004 Orange Revolution in Ukraine, in which the official CIS election monitoring team affirmed the victory of the pro-Russia candidate, and the more inconclusive 2005 Tulip Revolution in Kyrgyzstan. China, which is a major player it both security and economic questions in Central Asia, is, in contrast, relatively welcomed as it does not care about democratic shortcomings and can act as a balancer against Russia. Some, however, would maintain that would should not make too much of Russian-led "regionalism" in Central Asia, which is little more than a "thin layer of multilateralism still cloaked by bilateral agreements."[6]

Nonetheless, the CIS countries performed particularly well in the World Bank's "Doing Business 2016" survey, with nearly all countries within the region enjoying an increase in their ranking. As depicted in Figure 3.1, when indexed against 2010 scores, CIS countries, along with the CEE economies, have far outperformed the EU in terms of improvements in the distance to frontier (DTF) value from 0 to 100. Germany, on the other hand, got worse.

Russia missed out on entering the world's top 50 economies in the World Bank's "Doing Business 2016" survey, ranking 51st out of 189 countries. While President Vladimir Putin had targeted 50th slot this year, the position still marks an improvement on last year's assessment,

___

[6] Allison (2004, p. 470).

2010=100

CEE/CIS average Germany Russian Federation 156.5
EU average Kazakhstan Uzbekistan

140

129.2
127.4
120 120.5

106.0
100 99.9

2010   2011   2012   2013   2014   2015   2016

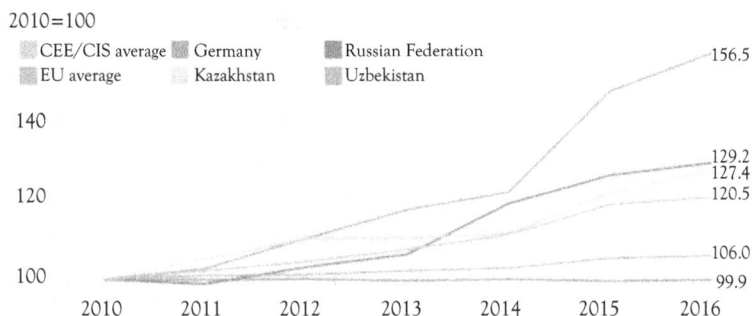

Figure 3.1 Change in DTF score for CIS countries, 2010–2014

Source: World Bank "Doing Business 2016."

which put Russia in 62nd place. In 2012, Putin promised that Russia would reach 20th in the World Bank's report by 2018. While this year's place is still some distance away, it is a vast improvement on previous years. In 2011 Russia sat all the way down in 120th place.

The strides being made are a vindication of Putin's efforts, and the breakdown by the World Bank of the reforms made by Moscow show that real efforts are being made to improve the business climate in the CEE and CIS's biggest economy. Russia this year improved in five key areas: Starting a business; getting electricity; registering property; and getting credit and paying taxes. These improvements, the report says, "were most successful in regions with greater government transparency" and "greater fiscal autonomy."

Kazakhstan also impressed in this year's report, climbing 12 places to 41st. Along with Russia, it was one of only 12 economies to implement 4 or more reforms since the last "Doing Business" report, at 7 and 5 reforms, respectively. Meanwhile, Ukraine jumped 13 places to 83rd slot, fulfilling President Petro Poroshenko's earlier pledge of a rise of "at least 10 places" in the ranking as a result of reforms carried out under his watch. Belarus also significantly improved its position, ranking 44th among the 189 countries, compared with 57th place the previous year.

Several are the challenges affecting the CIS economies. Aside from geo-political factors, the following are some important aspects to consider when entering these markets.

Skill Mismatches

Skill mismatches and skill shortages have become a priority concern for policy makers in many countries, especially since the onset of the global economic crisis and its intensification through the crisis in the Euro-zone. Endogenous growth models emphasize that human capital is a key resource for growth.[7] In fact, skill mismatch has an adverse effect on the efficiency of labor markets, particularly in transition economies, raising unemployment above the levels that could potentially be achieved given the level of aggregate demand. Efficient matching would reduce frictional and structural unemployment and ensure that vacancies are matched to workers with appropriate qualifications and skills.[8]

For instance, often lack of specialized education of the workforce translates into thwarted growth being curbed lack of a skilled workforce. Per models of endogenous growth,[9] the skill levels of the workforce, particularly in transition economies, are an important driver of economic development. This is partly due to different patterns of structural change and partly associated with demographic factors. Countries with high population growth rates may experience over—supply of educated school leavers; countries with falling populations may experience under-supply of both skilled and unskilled workers. There is also evidence of gender-biased mismatch in these markets. Among the main challenges to the development of effective skill matching systems and corresponding policy design in transition countries are weak capacities of government institutions including the employment services, underfunding of state provided training services, slow reforms of the education systems and low level of in-house training by employers.[10]

---

[7] Romer, P.M. 1994 "The origins of endogenous growth." *Journal of Economic Perspectives* 8, no. 1, pp. 3–22.

[8] Petrolongo, B., and C. Pissarides. 2001. "Looking into the Black Box: A Survey of the Matching Function." *Journal of Economic Literature* 39, pp. 390–431.

[9] Endogenous growth is long-run economic growth at a rate determined by forces that are internal to the economic system, particularly those forces governing the opportunities and incentives to create technological knowledge.

[10] Will, B. 2013. "Skill Mismatch, Education Systems, and Labor Markets in EU Neighborhood Policy Countries." Search, European Institute, http://ub.edu/search-project/wp-content/uploads/2013/09/WP05.20.pdf last accessed on 01/04/2016.

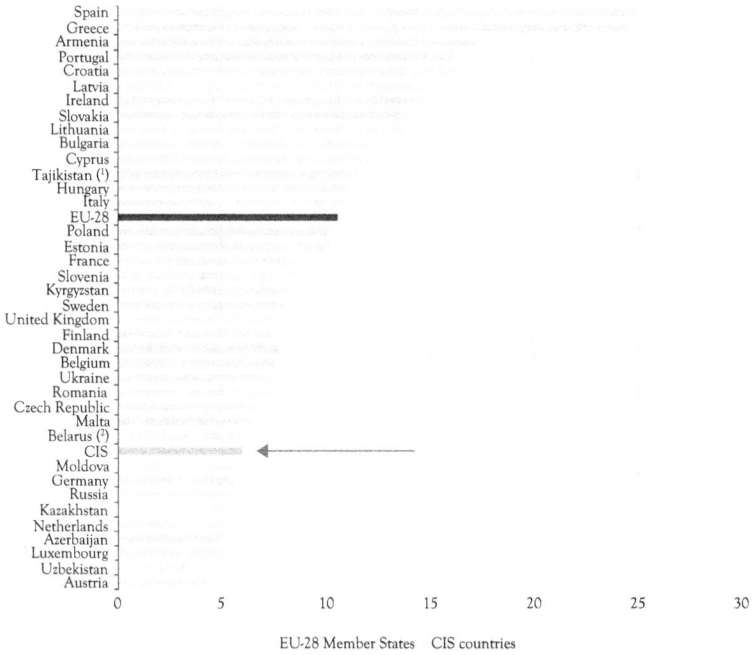

(¹) Data for 2009.
(²) According to the population census; 2009.

Figure 3.2 Unemployment rates for CIS countries and the region

Source: Eurostat and CIS-STAT.

Most of the CIS countries have experienced volatile labor markets for many years. For 2015, the share of employment in the primary sector in the CIS countries was larger than the EU-28 average by 9.9 percentage points (14.9 and 5.0 percent, respectively), while the share of employment in the tertiary (services) sector was smaller in the CIS countries (60.4 percent against 70.3 percent in the EU-28), as depicted in Figure 3.2.

Education System

Education systems in many CIS countries are still characterized by poor quality and irrelevance of much education provision in the region.[11] It is

---

[11] Sondergaard, L., and M. Murthi. 2012. *Skills, Not Just Diplomas: Managing Education for Results in the CIS and Central Asia*. Washington: The World Bank.

increasingly being recognized that curricula inherited from the previous communist system were unsuited to the development of a service-oriented post-Fordist[12] market economy and have not been upgraded sufficiently to reflect the new occupations that have emerged in the service sectors and in high technology industries. Skills that are taught in vocational education institutions tend to be too specialized in obsolete occupations. Education methods often outdated and dependent on rote learning, based on memorization techniques and repetition rather than problem solving. There is generally a deficit of education in transferable skills (so-called "soft skills").

Skills produced by the education system are often no longer demanded in the labor market. A recent study of the development of skills mismatches in the CIS found that

> even when people hold the correct qualification for an occupation they may not necessarily have the skills needed to effectively perform the job and satisfy employer expectations. Rapid technological and economic change makes difficult to predict what types of skills will be needed in the near and more distant future and what kinds of new jobs will appear.[13]

Moreover, because of structural change, it seems that skill mismatch is a more permanent phenomenon in the CIS markets than in the advanced economies resulting in high levels of long-term unemployment, and that skills mismatch increases with the age of workers, rather than falling as it does in the developed economies.

---

[12] Post-Fordism is the name given by some scholars to what they describe as the dominant system of economic production, consumption and associated socio-economic phenomena, in most industrialized countries since the late 20th century.

[13] ETF 2011. Labour Markets and Employability: Trends and Challenges in Armenia, Azerbaijan, Belarus, Georgia, Moldova and Ukraine. Turin: European Training Foundation; Eurostat 2010. Statistical Pocket Book for the Candidate and Potential Candidate Countries. Brussels: Eurostat, p. 229.

With falling school enrolment rates, deteriorating education quality and school systems struggling to overcome the global financial crisis, education is a top priority. Despite ongoing reforms, the region's under-resourced education systems are struggling to improve equity, quality, and governance. Children and adolescents face many barriers to school participation and learning.

Disparities in access persist for the hardest to reach groups, with policies and programs for minority groups showing little impact. Children with disabilities are almost entirely excluded from education, dropout rates are rising in many countries and, in some countries, primary school enrolment rates are declining. Families' costs of educating children have increased, especially considering the current financial crisis, which exacerbates existing barriers to access.

School quality is also declining, with low levels of learning achievement, inadequate teacher preparation systems, outdated teaching methodologies, over-centralized school governance, and crumbling school infrastructure among the major concerns. Early childhood education services are scarce and often do not serve those who would benefit the most. Ability tracking and segregation of children to special schools persist. Youth unemployment is often double and triple that of the national unemployment rate, partly because young people leave school without the skills needed to participate in today's knowledge economy.

Economic Restructuring

Skill shortages and surpluses of various types are a challenge for the CIS countries because of economic restructuring. We point out how in former Soviet-Countries structural changes in industrial organization are expected to afford directly the stability and functioning of the social fabric. Societal system is linked to production system through a specific network of linkages which substantially (qualitatively) differ from those we are acquainted with in the Western economies. The Soviet context is pivoted on the Soviet enterprises, an institution which keeps together linked State and Civil Society, Production and Reproduction, Economics and Policy, brief all those couples that in Western-Context a series of institutions try to keep rather separated.

In other words, the responsibility (commonwealth) that Soviet enterprises holds toward citizens is immediate and put under their own direct control: the enterprise provides them with everything they need for living, from cradle to the grave. The institutional framework has therefore remained extremely a simplified one: liability remains substantially concentrated in the hands of the enterprise, and is not split throughout a set of institutions. The main socio-economic guarantees were distributed through the Soviet enterprises and citizens enjoyed them through their belonging to the working communities who were entitled of enterprises operation management.

Accordingly, key functions concerning social citizenship where operated and channeled through the Soviet enterprises: from one side, the enterprise traditionally represented the main source of rights for citizens and, on the other one, citizens control and guarantees rested upon their property rights imbedded within the Soviet enterprises. In such a way, entrepreneurship in the Soviet context has maintained a striking association with social and moral responsibility. Within this oversimplified institutional framework, production could not emancipate from both its immediate social meaning and from related costs (sacrifices); and economic growth could not divorce from obligations related to social (community) development. Therefore, due to these specific features of the material constitution of the Soviet context, any changes occurring in production, organization of work, industrial organization, and so on, briefly, in the economic sphere, would affect immediately social life as a whole.

Legal Framework and Trading Policies

In the area of trade-related policies, the CIS countries will have to continue to make strategic decisions on policy objectives that have so far been avoided. Necessary adjustments to specific policy instruments will be limited and mostly technical in nature. Similarly, current plans for regional integration among CIS countries are fundamentally in compliance with WTO rules.

Negotiating strategies, however, will need to be carefully coordinated among CIS countries that are in a de facto, though not necessarily a de jure customs union. Systemic transformation, especially the imposition and further strengthening of financial discipline on formerly socialist enterprises through privatization and elimination of subsidies, will need to be carried forward vigorously. Benefits of WTO accession include the consolidation of recent improvements in market access and, above all else, greater credibility for market-oriented reform policies through the international commitments to be entered by CIS governments with respect to future trade-related policies.

Generally, regionalism, as opposed to multilateralism, is a centripetal process that involves the movement of two or more economies toward greater integration with one another. This process is driven either by political forces that are motivated by security, economic or other concerns or by microeconomic forces (such as firms, banks, people) often spurred by the pressure of competition. Whenever the first objectives dominate or are exclusive "de jure, regionalism" might occur. De jure regionalism takes a variety of institutional forms ranging from "free" or preferential trade agreements to customs unions or common markets and economic unions. These institutional arrangements have in common the exercise of extra-economic powers of state to lower barriers, especially policy barriers, to intra-regional economic activities. "De facto regionalism," in contrast, necessitates both the political will and the support from an economic constituency. It takes the form of significant cross-border trade and investment flows due to geographical and/or cultural proximity leading to growing regional integration. Whether either form of regionalism reinforces or jeopardizes the multilateral trading system remains an open question but it is likely that to some effects the balance of benefits may depend on the institutional form of agreements.

As for most industrialized countries trade volumes increased significantly in the period after World War II, trade has been identified as one potential culprit for the worsened position of low skilled workers.[14] Trade is thought to have affected the demand for low-skilled workers in two ways. It is thought to have reduced the relative demand for low-skilled labor and to have made the demand more responsive to changes in the price of low-skilled labor. Both effects would reduce the relative wages of

---

[14] Other factors that affect wage and/or employment inequalities are migration, technological change and changes in the skill distribution of the labor force.

low skilled workers in economies with flexible labor markets. In economies where labor market rigidities prevent wages from falling an increased relative unemployment rate of low-skilled labor may result. Country-specific labor market characteristics would thus have an important effect on whether and to which extent relative wages and trade affects relative unemployment rates.

Does all this mean that foreign investors should avoid trading with or investing in the CIS markets? On the contrary, however, any organized program of opening to the CIS markets must include specialized expertise, on-the-ground knowledge, local partnerships and, most of all, patience.

Why Multinationals Fail in the CIS Markets?

Pacek and Thorniley[15] identified an exhaustive range of factors contributing to the failure of companies from advanced economies into the CIS markets. These factors may be divided into external and internal factors and almost all are related to strategic and leadership issues:

- Leaders fail to consider CIS markets as an integral part of strategy and acknowledge that such markets need to be approached with a distinct set of criteria for judging progress and success.
- Top leaders fail to commit sufficient resources to get businesses established and growing in CIS markets, or acknowledge that it is never a short-term affair.
- Multinational enterprises (MNEs) fail to appoint a head manager for CIS markets and often assign this responsibility to an international manager who is responsible for markets in both advanced and emerging markets. The problem with this is that operational approaches are distinct in each of these markets.

---

[15] Pacek, N., and D. Thorniley. 2007. *The CIS Markets: Lessons for Business and the Outlook for Different Markets.* 2nd ed. London: The Economist and Profile Books.

- MNEs fail to understand that business is driven by heads of regions and business units rather than by heads of functional areas. While the former has a focus and appreciation for the CIS economies the latter tend also to be interested in advanced markets.
- MNEs do not acknowledge that CIS markets operate under distinct business models and structures, and often merely transfer practices tested in advanced economies without considering adaptation.
- The board members of many MNEs have limited diversity in terms of culture and ethnic background and do not develop sufficient appreciation for the peculiarities of the CIS markets.
- MNEs underestimate the potential and often early competition from smaller international and domestic companies, thus never accepting that they may be destined as a follower in CIS markets.
- Economic and political crisis also exist in CIS markets, as discussed earlier, and have a significant impact on business performance. Top managers need to understand this, be prepared to adapt and introduce new tactics rather than changing strategy, which despite having short-term success, tends to be the wrong approach in the long-term.
- MNEs get alarmed by short-term slippages and cut costs to attain favorable temporary results, yet this is likely to have a structural impact on strategy implementation and long-term results.
- MNEs set unrealistic targets to achieve, which leave managers with limited maneuvering space and short-lived careers.
- MNEs fail to recognize that entering the market early is fundamental in establishing networks, developing brands and learning the larger context from which it will operate.
- Senior leaders fail to recognize that developing a network of reliable contacts often requires establishing friendships with locals, which requires time and visibility in CIS markets.
- MNEs fail to empower regional and country managers and delegate decision-making power to local managers.

- Foreign companies fail to recognize that CIS markets are more price-sensitive and often stick to their pricing structures instead of adapting to local sensitivities.
- International enterprises fail to recognize that their product portfolio is not tailored to the lower and middle segments of emergent markets and do not develop innovations that are context oriented.
- Foreign enterprises underestimate the competition from local companies in emergent markets, which gradually move from up from lower to upper segments. Local companies understand better than anyone about local markets, sometimes employ dubious practices, and often have the support of local governments.
- One of the largest obstacles that foreign companies face may be the unwillingness to change long-standing business practices.
- Another challenge is to appoint senior managers who are not familiar with the local market, culture, and language in emerging countries.
- The fact that demand is volatile and unpredictable in emerging and frontier markets may discourage multinationals, which often expect reliable market information.

The failure factors are numerous and diverse but as Pacek and Thorniley noted it all boils down to a lack of adequate market entry preparation. Preparation requires companies to continuously research the external environment and know how to use internal resources to take advantage of opportunities. Hence, a preliminary audit that focuses on external and internal factors is essential. The external factors may be examined by posing questions concerning the market, the political environment, the economic environment, and the business environment, as depicted in Table 3.1.

By the same token, the internal factors must inquire about resources, products, organization, and risks, as depicted in Table 3.2.

Having done a preliminary external and internal audit, managers need to prepare a business proposal describing what to do, how to do

Table 3.1 External factors and sample questions

Understanding the market	
Market potential	• How large and wealthy is the market? • Is there unsatisfied demand for the product/service?
Understanding local consumers/customers	• Who are the consumers/customers? What are their characteristics? • How do consumers make their decisions?
Reaching the consumer/customer	• How difficult/easy is it to reach potential consumers/customers? • How do competitors and noncompetitors reach their customers?
Competition	• Which competitors are already operating in the market? • How strong are these competitors?
Lessons learned by noncompetitors	• What do noncompetitors say about the business environment in the country? • What have been the largest obstacles to successful operations?
Local culture	• What aspects of local culture are relevant to running a successful local business?
Understanding the political and economic environment	
Economic outlook	• How sustainable is economic growth? • What is driving economic growth?
Political outlook	• What is the level of political risk and how will or might affect the business?
Government policies	• Does the government allow a level-playing field? • Is the government in the hands of local lobbies?
Understanding the business environment	
Finance	• Is it possible to finance operations locally? • What access do customers/consumers have to finance?
Labor market	• What are the wage/salary rates for the employees who will be needed? • What are the most effective ways of recruiting local employees?
Taxation	• What are the current levels of taxation? • What is the outlook for tax incentives?
Legal environment	• How effective and efficient is the local judiciary? • Is there any hope that the legal system will improve?
Bureaucratic obstacles to business	• What are the most common bureaucratic obstacles for business? • How easy or difficult it is to set up business in the country?

(Continued)

Table 3.1 External factors and sample questions   (Continued)

Crime and corruption	• Is crime a problem for business? • What is the level of corruption?
Infrastructure	• What is the quality of local transport infrastructure? • And telecommunications?
Foreign trade environment	• Is the country a WTO member? • Does it belong to any trading blocs or regional free-trade areas?
Cost of building a business and brand	• How expensive is it to build a brand? • How much time will it take to do what is necessary to get the business off the ground?

Table 3.2 Internal factors and sample questions

Resources	• How much time and money will be required? • Is the CEO committed to support business development and provide necessary resources? And the senior managers? • What human resources are needed?
Products	• Is the product portfolio right for the market? • Will investment be available for developing new products?
Organization	• Could existing internal processes and operational practices help or hinder what is planned? • What existing capabilities can be drawn?
Risks	• Can the risks that have been identified be managed? • How would entry be financed?

it, by when, and resources required. Business must then ask themselves whether there are similar or better opportunities available in other CIS markets. How then, can we compare the potential of different CIS markets?

Best Opportunities Fill in Institutional Voids

From an institutional viewpoint, the market is a transactional place embedded in information and property rights, and CIS markets are a place where one or both features are underdeveloped.[16] Most definitions of CIS markets are descriptive based on poverty and growth indicators, and their economic *stage*. In contrast, a structural definition as proposed by Khanna and Palepu points to issues that are problematic therefore allowing an immediate identification of solutions. Moreover, a structural definition allows us not only to understand commonalities among CIS markets but also to understand what differentiates each of these markets. Finally, a structural approach provides a more precise understanding of the market dynamics that genuinely differentiates the CIS markets from advanced economies.

To illustrate, let us contrast the equity capital markets of South Korea and Chile. As per the International Finance Corporation (IFC) definition, South Korea is not an emerging market because it is an OECD member, however when we look at its equity capital market we notice that until recently it was not functioning well, in other words it has an institutional void. Chile on the other hand is considered an emerging market in Latin America but it has an efficient capital market, thus no institutional void appears in this sector. However, Chile has institutional voids in other markets such as the products market. Similar factors exist among CIS countries.

Strategy formulation in CIS markets, therefore, must begin with a map of institutional voids. What works in the headquarters of a multinational enterprise does not per se work in new locations with different institutional environments. The most common mistake companies do when entering CIS markets is to overestimate the importance of past experience.

This common error reflects a recency bias: a person assumes that recent successful experiences may be transferred to other places. A manager may incorrectly assume that the way people are motivated in one country would be the same in the new country (context). It may be assumed that everyone likes to be appreciated, but the way of expressing appreciation depends on the institutional environment. Khanna and Palepu point out that the human element is the cornerstone of operating in new contexts.

---

[16] Ibidem.

Ultimately, human beings, who provide a mix of history, culture, and interactions, create institutions.

In short, based on Khanna and Palepu's institutional approach to CIS markets it is necessary to answer several questions, including but not limited to:

- Which institutions are working and missing?
- Which parts of our business model (in the home country) would be affected by these voids?
- How can we build competitive advantage based on our ability to navigate institutional voids?
- How can we profit from the structural reality of CIS markets today by identifying opportunities to fill voids, serving as market intermediaries?

Strategies for CIS Markets

The work of Khanna and Palepu indicate that there are four generic strategic choices for companies operating in emerging markets, which also applies for CIS markets:

- Replicate or adapt?
- Compete alone or collaborate?
- Accept or attempt to change market context?
- Enter, wait, or exit?

The CIS markets attract two competing types of enterprises, the developed market-based multinationals and the emerging market-based companies. Both bring different advantages to fill institutional voids. MNEs bring brands, capital talent, and resources, such as the case of several ones based in Lithuania, whereas local companies contribute with local contacts and context knowledge. Because they have different strengths and resources, foreign and domestic firms will compete differently and must develop strategies accordingly. Table 3.3 summarizes the strategies and options for both MNCs and local companies.

Table 3.3 Responding to institutional voids

Strategic choice	Options for MNCs from developed countries	Options for the CISan market-based companies
Replicate or adapt?	• Replicate business model, exploiting relative advantage of global brand, credibility, know-how, talent, finance, and other factor inputs. • Adapt business models, products, or organizations to institutional voids.	• Copy business model from developed countries. • Exploit local knowledge, capabilities, and ability to navigate institutional voids to build tailored business models.
Compete alone or collaborate?	• Compete alone. • Acquire capabilities to navigate institutional voids through local partnerships or joint ventures (JVs).	• Compete alone. • Acquire capabilities from developed markets through partnerships or JVs with multinational companies to bypass institutional voids.
Accept or attempt to change market context?	• Take market context as given. • Fill institutional voids in service of own business.	• Take market context as given. • Fill institutional voids in service of own business.
Enter, wait, or exit?	• Enter or stay in market spite of institutional voids. • Emphasize opportunities elsewhere.	• Build business in home market in spite of institutional voids. • Exit home market early in corporate history if capabilities unrewarded at home.

Source: Khanna and Palepu (2010).

Anand P. Arkalgud[17] provides a good example of how companies fill institutional voids. Take the example of India, where road infrastructure is still underdeveloped in terms of quality and connectivity. Traditionally Tata Motors has been the dominant player in the auto industry but when it started to receive competition from Volvo in the truck segment and by Japanese auto makers in the car segment Tata responded. It created a mini-truck that not only provided more capacity and safety than the

---

[17] Arnand Prasad Arkalgud (September 9, 2011) Filling "institutional voids" in emerging markets. *Forbes magazine.* http://forbes.com/sites/infosys/2011/09/20/filling-institutional-voids-in-emerging-markets/ Last accessed on 12/15/2015.

two- and three-wheeled pollutant vehicles used to access market areas but also an environmentally sound vehicle, one that could easily maneuver U-turns in such narrow streets.

Another case in India involved Coca Cola, who discovered that their beverages were being sold "warm." Coca Cola realized that it needed a solution to sell its product "chilled." The reason for the warm bottles was that electricity supplies in these remote locations were unstable especially in summer periods, not allowing the bottles to remain chilled. Thus the company developed a solar-powered cooler and partnered with a local refrigeration company.

Tarun Khanna and Krishna Palepu propose the following five contexts as a framework in assessing the institutional environment of any country. The five contexts include the markets needed to acquire input (product, labor, and capital), and markets needed to sell output. This is referred to as the products and services market. In addition to these three dimensions the framework includes a broader sociopolitical context defined by political and social systems and degrees of openness. When applying the framework, managers need to ask a set of questions in each dimension. An example of these questions is indicated in Table 3.4 below.

Table 3.4 Framework to assess institutional voids

Institutional dimension	Questions
Product markets	1. Can companies easily obtain reliable data on customer tastes and purchase behaviors? Are there cultural barriers to market research? Do world-class market research firms operate in the country? 2. Can consumers easily obtain unbiased information on the quality of the goods and services they want to buy? Are there independent consumer organizations and publications that provide such information? 3. Can company's access raw materials and components of good quality? Is there a deep network of suppliers? Are there firms that assess suppliers' quality and reliability? Can companies enforce contracts with suppliers? 4. How strong are the logistics and transportation infrastructures? Have global logistics companies set up local operations? 5. Do large retail chains exist in the country? If so, do they cover the entire country or only the major cities? Do they reach all consumers or only wealthy ones?

	6. Are there other types of distribution channels, such as direct-to-consumer channels and discount retail channels that deliver products to customers? 7. Is it difficult for multinationals to collect receivables from local retailers? 8. Do consumers use credit cards, or does cash dominate transactions? Can consumers get credit to make purchases? Are data on customer creditworthiness available? 9. What recourse do consumers have against false claims by companies or defective products and services? 10. How do companies deliver after-sales service to consumers? Is it possible to set up a nationwide service network? Are third-party service providers reliable? 11. Are consumers willing to try new products and services? Do they trust goods from local companies? How about from foreign companies? 12. What kind of product-related environmental and safety regulations are in place? How do the authorities enforce those regulations?
Labor markets	1. How strong is the country's education infrastructure, especially for technical and management training? Does it have a good elementary and secondary education system as well? 2. Do people study and do business in English or in another international language, or do they mainly speak a local language? 3. Are data available to help sort out the quality of the country's educational institutions? 4. Can employees move easily from one company to another? Does the local culture support that movement? Do recruitment agencies facilitate executive mobility? 5. What are the major post recruitment-training needs of the people that multinationals hire locally? 6. Is pay for performance a standard practice? How much weight do executives give seniority, as opposed to merit, in making promotion decisions? 7. Would a company be able to enforce employment contracts with senior executives? Could it protect itself against executives who leave the firm and then compete against it? Could it stop employees from stealing trade secrets and intellectual property? 8. Does the local culture accept foreign managers? Do the laws allow a firm to transfer locally hired people to another country? Do managers want to stay or leave the nation? 9. How are the rights of workers protected? How strong are the country's trade unions? Do they defend workers' interests or only advance a political agenda? 10. Can companies use stock options and stock-based compensation schemes to motivate employees? 11. Do the laws and regulations limit a firm's ability to restructure, downsize, or shut down?

(Continued)

Table 3.4 Framework to assess institutional voids   *(Continued)*

Institutional dimension	Questions
	12. If a company were to adopt its local rivals' or suppliers' business practices, such as the use of child labor, would that tarnish its image overseas?
Capital markets	1. How effective are the country's banks, insurance companies, and mutual funds at collecting savings and channeling them into investments?
	2. Are financial institutions managed well? Is their decision making transparent? Do noneconomic considerations, such as family ties, influence their investment decisions?
	3. Can companies raise large amounts of equity capital in the stock market? Is there a market for corporate debt?
	4. Does a venture capital industry exist? If so, does it allow individuals with good ideas to raise funds?
	5. How reliable are sources of information on company performance? Do the accounting standards and disclosure regulations permit investors and creditors to monitor company management?
	6. Do independent financial analysts, rating agencies, and the media offer unbiased information on companies?
	7. How effective are corporate governance norms and standards at protecting shareholder interests?
	8. Are corporate boards independent and empowered, and do they have independent directors?
	9. Are regulators effective at monitoring the banking industry and stock markets?
	10. How well do the courts deal with fraud?
	11. Do the laws permit companies to engage in hostile takeovers? Can shareholders organize themselves to remove entrenched managers through proxy fights?
	12. Is there an orderly bankruptcy process that balances the interests of owners, creditors, and other stakeholders?
Political and social system	1. To whom are the country's politicians accountable? Are there strong political groups that oppose the ruling party? Do elections take place regularly?
	2. Are the roles of the legislative, executive, and judiciary clearly defined? What is the distribution of power between the central, state, and city governments?
	3. Does the government go beyond regulating business to interfering in it or running companies?
	4. Do the laws articulate and protect private property rights?
	5. What is the quality of the country's bureaucrats? What are bureaucrats' incentives and career trajectories?
	6. Is the judiciary independent? Do the courts adjudicate disputes and enforce contracts in a timely and impartial manner? How effective are the quasi judicial regulatory institutions that set and enforce rules for business activities?

	7. Do religious, linguistic, regional, and ethnic groups coexist peacefully, or are there tensions between them?
	8. How vibrant and independent is the media? Are newspapers and magazines neutral, or do they represent sectarian interests?
	9. Are nongovernmental organizations, civil rights groups, and environmental groups active in the country?
	10. Do people tolerate corruption in business and government?
	11. What role do family ties play in business?
	12. Can strangers be trusted to honor a contract in the country?
Openness	1. Are the country's government, media, and people receptive to foreign investment? Do citizens trust companies and individuals from some parts of the world more than others?
	2. What restrictions does the government place on foreign investment? Are those restrictions in place to facilitate the growth of domestic companies, to protect state monopolies, or because people are suspicious of multinationals?
	3. Can a company make greenfield investments and acquire local companies, or can it only break into the market by entering into joint ventures? Will that company be free to choose partners based purely on economic considerations?
	4. Does the country allow the presence of foreign intermediaries such as market research and advertising firms, retailers, media companies, banks, insurance companies, venture capital firms, auditing firms, management consulting firms, and educational institutions?
	5. How long does it take to start a new venture in the country? How cumbersome are the government's procedures for permitting the launch of a wholly foreign-owned business?
	6. Are there restrictions on portfolio investments by overseas companies or on dividend repatriation by multinationals?
	7. Does the market drive exchange rates, or does the government control them? If it's the latter, does the government try to maintain a stable exchange rate, or does it try to favor domestic products over imports by propping up the local currency?
	8. What would be the impact of tariffs on a company's capital goods and raw materials imports? How would import duties affect that company's ability to manufacture its products locally versus exporting them from home?
	9. Can a company set up its business anywhere in the country? If the government restricts the company's location choices, are its motives political, or is it inspired by a logical regional development strategy?
	10. Has the country signed free-trade agreements with other nations? If so, do those agreements favor investments by companies from some parts of the world over others?
	11. Does the government allow foreign executives to enter and leave the country freely? How difficult is it to get work permits for managers and engineers?
	12. Does the country allow its citizens to travel abroad freely? Can ideas flow into the country unrestricted? Are people permitted to debate and accept those ideas?

Conclusion

Entry mode[18] is determined by product, market and organizational factors. Regarding products and services, MNEs need to know whether the nature and range of the product or service, along with available marketing strategies will require any adaptation. If so, they should consider a partner in the CIS country they plan to enter. Usually a higher level of control and resource commitment in the foreign market is required for new or wider product offerings as well as higher levels of adaptation. When considering market factors managers need to consider physical distance and experience, as well as identify appropriate marketing strategies and distribution channels, and priorities in revenues, costs, and profits.

Organizationally, major concerns are communication with foreign operations and control of overseas activities. One concern in foreign markets is the control of assets. Firms will prefer to internalize activities in where there is a higher chance of opportunism by the partners in those markets.

For CIS, the region is poised for further growth, but some major obstacles remain on the road to prosperity. Chief among them are social and economic tensions between ethnic groups, which can create problems ranging from labor markets conflicts to security risks for local businesses. Such dynamics are a special concern during periods of economic distress, high unemployment and political unrest—known causes of nationalistic, antioutsider fervor.

Russia should not be underestimated as it plays an important role in the economies of the CIS. And Vladimir Putin has been frank about his ambition to create a Eurasian economic union, composed mainly of former Soviet states, as a counterweight to the EU. The long-term possibility of new realignments, this time toward the East, cannot be dismissed.

A case in point, most recently, the developments in Crimea have shown that despite years of change and effort toward global integration, Russian strategic goals in the region should not be overlooked. Putin's rule, reminiscent of the iron hands that governed Russia during the Soviet era, coupled with those weakened by the *Great Recession* in the West, is a recipe for a meal that's only served very cold.

---

[18] http://globaledge.msu.edu/reference-desk/online-course-modules/market-research-and-entry

CHAPTER 4

The Impact of the Global Economic Crisis on CIS Economies

Overview

Emerging market economies, including the CIS countries, were major beneficiaries of the economic boom before 2007. Nonetheless, they have become victims of the global financial crisis. Their future development depends, to a larger extent, on global economic prospects. Today the global economy and the European economy are much more integrated and interdependent than they were 10 or 20 years ago. Every country must recognize its limited economic sovereignty and must be prepared to deal with the consequences of global macroeconomic fluctuations.

Overall, the CIS countries, excluding Russia, have been generally badly affected by the global financial crisis and economic downturn in 2008. The impact on growth has varied but weak demand for commodities and exports, as well as the drying-up of international liquidity had significant repercussions. CIS countries were particularly affected by commodity prices, which fell because of slowing global demand. Ukraine, for instance, is highly dependent on steel. Similarly, oil-rich central Asian countries such as Kazakhstan were affected in a similar way.

As a result of the global financial crisis, emerging and developing economies across the globe experienced a sharp slowdown in output growth. In aggregate, real gross domestic product (GDP) growth in emerging and developing economies fell from 8.3 percent in 2007 to 6.1 percent in 2008 and just 1.2 percent in 2015 (IMF 2016). Commodity concentration was a problem for many of the CIS and is the result of their minimal production and export of manufactured goods and heavy reliance on commodity exports, primarily oil and gas.

Global Economic Crisis Impact on CIS Economies

On average, the CEE region experienced a smaller output decline than the Euro area and the entire EU while the CIS, especially its European part, contracted more dramatically. However, there was a deep differentiation within each country group. Looking globally, richer countries, which are more open to trade and in which the banking sector plays a larger role and which rely more on external financing, suffered more than less-sophisticated economies, which are less dependent on trade and credit. With some exceptions, the previous good growth performance helped rather than handicapped countries in the CIS regions in the crisis year of 2009.

CIS countries which had no EU membership perspective, or even close association, benefited from the global commodity boom. All post-communist economies gained from the previous decade of painful economic reforms and restructuring. But with the inception of the global financial crisis, liquidity and credit dried up, capital started to leave the CIS region and fly back to the main financial centers, mostly the U.S. Stock markets and commodity prices declined, although there was almost a 1-year time mismatch between the collapse of these two asset markets, risk premia for both sovereign and private borrowing grew dramatically, and many national currencies depreciated, especially in countries which run floating exchange rate regimes, threatening the massive insolvency of economic agents borrowing in foreign currencies.

Some countries experienced banking sector troubles. Few financial institutions in the CIS were directly affected by the U.S. subprime mortgage crisis, thanks to their comparatively small exposure to overseas assets. However, financial institutions were far from immune. Banks in Kazakhstan, Central Asia's largest economy, were thought to be particularly badly affected as they borrowed heavily from foreign institutions, including those in the United States, and were overexposed to the domestic construction sector which experienced a sharp downturn immediately after the crisis started. But these Central Asian countries seemed to be better insulated than the CEE countries. For instance, windfall oil revenues had allowed Kazakhstan to build up estimated foreign exchange reserves of $16.8 billion in 2008, and in October 2008 the government had announced it was going to spend $5 billion to recapitalize struggling banks.

During the financial crisis, some sectors were more impacted than others. The uncertainty during the crisis caused consumers and businesses to postpone discretionary purchases, of which consumer durables and investment goods are the most important. In addition, these types of products are much more likely to be bought on credit than consumption nondurables, and once capital markets froze, financing was no longer available. In some countries, especially those with housing bubbles, the construction sector was also severely impacted.

The resource rich CIS, which includes Russia, had surpluses of over 10 percent of GDP going into the crisis and although these fell slightly in 2009 due to the fall in commodity prices early in that year, the surpluses were expected to start growing again in the following year. However, one should realize that although the CIS economies had overall current account surpluses, their private financial sectors were heavily dependent on external capital inflows. Thus, the dependence of the region on foreign capital to finance their future development was one of the most significant medium-run consequences of the current global economic crisis.

Some banks have failed during the crisis. In Russia about 20 banks failed. The government provided bailouts to systemically or regionally important banks. Depositors were generally protected and have not lost their money as they did in some previous crises. However, there were some minor problems, such as in Ukraine, where there were restrictions on bank withdrawals for a time. In a few cases, however, foreign bond holders or bank syndicates have had to take a haircut.

One simple way to gauge the effect of the crisis on CIS economies is to compare GDP growth over the period 2003 through 2007 with growth in 2008, 2009, and 2010, as outlined in Table 4.1. This suggests a shortfall of 1.3 percent in 2008, 5 percent in 2009, and 1.1 percent in 2010—or a cumulative loss of around 7.5 percent by 2010. The CIS region experienced a drop from 7.9 percent in 2003 to -6.6 percent in 2009, a total drop of 14.6 percent.

In the CIS, six of its economies, including Armenia, Belarus, Georgia, Kyrgyzstan, Tajikistan, and Ukraine, had to resort to IMF assistance in the second half of 2008 and the beginning of 2009 to secure their international liquidity and avoid both sovereign default and an uncontrolled run on their currencies. Turkmenistan and Uzbekistan, two of the least

Table 4.1 GDP growth in emerging and developing economies (percent)

Region	GDP Growth				Difference from 2003–07		
	2003 –07	2008	2009	2010	2008	2009	2010
All	7.4	6.1	2.4	6.3	-1.3	-5.0	-1.1
CEE	6.0	3.0	-3.7	2.8	-3.0	-9.7	-3.2
CIS	7.9	5.5	-6.6	4.0	-2.4	-14.6	-4.0
Developing Asia	9.2	7.9	6.6	8.7	-1.4	-2.6	-0.5
MENA	5.9	5.1	2.4	4.5	-0.8	-3.4	-1.4
Sub-Saharan Africa	6.3	5.5	2.1	4.7	-0.8	-4.2	-1.6
Western Hemisphere	4.9	4.3	-1.8	4.0	-0.6	-6.6	-0.9

Source: IMF (2010).

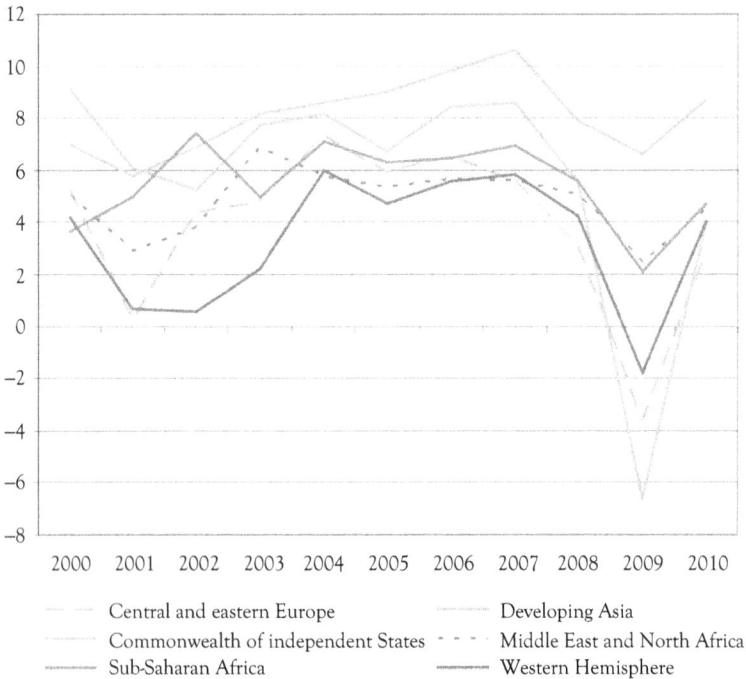

Figure 4.1 Real GDP growth in emerging and developing economies (percent)

Source: IMF.

developed countries in the region, were better insulated due to their weaker international financial and trade links, but still were more affected than initially thought.

As depicted on Figure 4.1, the real GDP of countries in the CIS, central and eastern Europe (CEE) and the Western Hemisphere contracted in

2009, while in developing Asia, sub-Saharan Africa, and the Middle East and North Africa (MENA) real GDP growth in 2009 was well below its average rate in the years leading up to the crisis.

Challenges and Implications

When it became clear that the crisis hit most emerging markets heavily, especially former communist economies in CEE and CIS, the previously optimistic forecasts gave way to alarming expectations and comments like that of the World Bank President Robert Zoellick's on February 27, 2009.[1] Even greater differences were observed within the CIS, as depicted in Table 4.2, where Ukraine contracted by 15.1 percent, Armenia by 14.4 percent, Russia by 7.9 percent, and Moldova by 6.5 percent. On the other hand, all 5 Central Asian countries, Azerbaijan, and Belarus continued growing, in some cases, Azerbaijan and Uzbekistan, at a pretty high rate. The CIS economies were the most impacted, dropping below -6 percent, but were also the ones to most aggressively recover, back to par with all other economic groups, except to developing Asia. Fortunately, these fears proved to be a bit exaggerated.

Clearly, all regions were badly affected. Countries in the CIS, as well as emerging economies in Asia, central and eastern Europe suffered the biggest falls in exports in 2009, both in absolute terms and relative to

Table 4.2 Annual growth of real GDP, in percent, 2003–2010, CIS

Country	2003	2004	2005	2006	2007	2008	2009	2010
Armenia	14.0	10.5	13.9	13.2	13.7	6.8	-14.4	1.8
Azerbaijan	10.5	10.2	26.4	34.5	25.0	10.8	9.3	2.7
Belarus	7.0	11.5	9.4	10.0	8.6	10.0	0.2	2.4
Georgia	11.1	5.9	9.6	9.4	12.3	2.3	-4.0	2.0
Kazakhstan	9.3	9.6	9.7	10.7	8.9	3.2	1.2	2.4
Kyrgyzstan	7.0	7.0	-0.2	3.1	8.5	8.4	2.3	4.6
Moldova	6.6	7.4	7.5	4.8	3.0	7.8	-6.5	2.5
Russia	7.3	7.2	6.4	7.7	8.1	5.6	-7.9	4.3
Tajikistan	10.2	10.6	6.7	7.0	7.8	7.9	3.4	4.0
Turkmenistan	17.1	14.7	13.0	11.4	11.6	10.5	4.2	12.0
Ukraine	9.6	12.1	2.7	7.3	7.9	2.1	-15.1	3.7
Uzbekistan	4.2	7.7	7.0	7.3	9.5	9.0	8.1	8.0

Source: International Monetary Fund, World Economic Outlook Database, April 2010.

---

[1] http://ft.com/cms/3cf2381c-c064-11dd-9559-000077b07658.html

expectations, but even sub-Saharan Africa, which is less well integrated into the global economy, experienced a fall of 7 percent in exports in 2009.[2]

The effect of the crisis on private capital flows was another important factor as CIS countries were severely impacted, seeing some large inflows in 2007 replaced by large outflows in 2008 and 2009. The biggest increases and subsequent declines in capital flows were in portfolio and other financial flows. Direct investment flows were boosted in 2007 and 2008, probably due mainly to extraordinary increases in some commodity prices. They have subsequently fallen back, but look set to remain above their 2006 level.

The regions most badly hit by the freezing of credit markets and a consequent drying up of capital inflows were the CIS countries and central and eastern Europe. This led to what are best described as depressions in the region, where GDP contracted by between 14 and 18 percent in 2009, and to severe recessions in many other economies.

When one limits the analyzed cross-country panel to Europe and CIS, the correlations remain the same in terms of direction but not in terms of strength. Three of the aforementioned correlations—between the growth rate of real GDP in 2009 and GDP PPP per capita level in 2006, exports-to-GDP ratio in 2006 and domestic credit-to-GDP ratio in 2006 are negative but weaker for Europe and CIS than globally. The same concerns the positive correlation between the 2009 growth rate and the average growth rate in 2003 to 2007, which is weaker for Europe and the CIS. However, another positive correlation—between the 2009 growth rate and the average current account balance in 2005 to 2007—proved to be stronger for Europe and the CIS than globally.

Economic Prospects

There is little prospect of growth in the CIS region returning to its pre-crisis level any time soon and unemployment will remain high for many

---

[2] It is not the focus of this chapter, not this book, for comprehensive analysis of the effects on individual countries. The Overseas Development Institute has examined the impact of the crisis on selected economies (ODI 2010).

years. This is almost certain to lead to *hysteresis effects*, or what economists refer to as the risk of some cyclical effects, such as an increase in unemployment during a recession, become more permanent, or structural. For example, workers who are unemployed in the CIS region for any length of time may lose the skills they need to find employment or find it difficult to acquire new skills that may be needed to find a job. Thus, they may settle for employment that is less productive than what they are capable of, or they may drop out of the labor force altogether. The economy's productive potential is, therefore, diminished.

Russia also experienced a sharp fall in capital in inflows in 2008 and 2009. These had been boosted ahead of the crisis by the high price of oil but fell away as the crisis developed. This had a very significant effect on the Russian economy, but also on the economies of many other countries in the CIS which had come to rely on exports to and remittance flows from Russia. We need to be careful, however, before attributing the problems of the CIS countries to the financial crisis alone. The exceptionally strong growth rates recorded there in the mid-2000s were, with the benefit of hindsight, unsustainable and only achievable because of some of the activities that ultimately caused the crisis.

Going beyond these general observations would require an analysis of structural data (e.g., the share of various sectors and industries) which are not available in terms of a cross-country comparative dataset. The only available figure of this kind, the average growth rate of the group of fuel exporters, indicates that they were more heavily hit in 2009 than other economies. Some anecdotal evidence may suggest that large shares of the construction, metallurgy, the automobile industries or the financial sector made the recent recession more severe.

On average, CIS countries have the chance to grow faster than the Euro area and the entire EU. This gives them the opportunity to continue the catching up process, although at a slower pace than during the boom preceding the recent crisis. However, the picture will be uneven within each regional group or subgroup as it was in 2009. And returning to the precrisis boom does not seem likely at least in the near future. In addition, the overall macroeconomic environment will be less comfortable, with higher debt-to-GDP ratios in most countries, and tighter credit conditions.

CHAPTER 5

Political Risk in CIS Region

Overview

The decision of whether or not to invest in foreign markets should include an assessment of the political environment. Political discontinuities create a level of uncertainty for companies and individuals because they can lead to significant shifts in policies, regulations, governmental administration, and other potential risk factors that are not typically associated with advanced economies. Political instability can lead to restrictions on products, technology, and labor and even lead to practices of discrimination against foreign firms. This chapter will survey the impact of a series of political and economic risk assessments that include factors such as economic growth, labor unrest, social unrest, armed conflict, and how those elements interact with local investments and foreign direct investment (FDI).

The Relevance of Risk

The reader might wonder why assess democratic governance in relation to political risk. A new field in political science has emerged which attempts to explore greater connections between these two phenomena. There is a renewed interest in how the political risk affects multinational corporations operating in emerging markets, and much of the research has focused on the relationship between democratic institutions and the flow of FDI. Nathan Jensen finds, for example, the democratic regimes reduce risks for multinational investors, specifically through increasing constraints on the executive.[1]

Table 5.1 provides data across a series of rankings of political risk for Commonwealth of Independent States (CIS) states and nearby territories

---

[1] Jensen (2008).

Table 5.1 Country ranking by political risk

Country	Rating	Political Rights	Civil Liberties	Freedom Rating
Armenia	Partly Free (61)	3	3	3
Azerbaijan	Not Free (16)	7	6	6.5
Belarus	Not Free (17)	7	6	6.5
Georgia	Partly Free (64)	3	3	3
Kazakhstan	Not Free (24)	6	5	5.5
Kyrgyzstan	Partly Free (38)	5	5	5
Moldova	Partly Free (60)	3	3	3
Russia	Not Free (22)	6	6	6
Tajikistan	Not Free (16)	7	6	6.5
Turkmenistan	Not Free (4)	7	7	7
Ukraine	Partly Free (61)	3	3	3
Uzbekistan	Not Free (3)	7	7	7

Note: The Democracy Scores are rated on a scale of 0=Worst and 100=Best, and regime ratings are based on a scale of 1 to 7, with 1 representing the highest level of democratic progress and 7 the lowest. The 2016 ratings reflect the period January 1 through December 31, 2015.[2]

in the region based on Freedom House indixes. Countries are rated on a scale of 1 to 7, with 1 representing the highest and 7 the lowest level of democratic progress. The average rating across the categories of "Electoral Process," "Civil Society," "Independent Media," "National Democratic Governance," "Local Democratic Governance," "Judicial Framework and Independence," and "Corruption" are used to create the overall country score. Each ranking is calculated using a series of variables derived from the most recent political data available (as of 2015 to 2016).

---

[2] *Nations is Transition* is the only comprehensive, comparative, and multidimensional study of reform in the former Communist states of Europe and Eurasia. Nations in Transition tracks the reform record of 29 countries and administrative areas and provides Freedom House's most in-depth data about this vast and important region. The 2014 edition covers events from January 1 through December 31, 2013. It is an updated edition of surveys published in 2013, 2012, 2011, 2010, 2009, 2008, 2007, 2006, 2005, 2004, 2003, 2002, 2001, 1999, 2000, 1998, 1997, and 1995. For information, see www.freedomhouse.org/report-types/nations-transit#.VdSJr86lSLg

These relationships, and the variables noted in the Freedom House rankings, will be explored in more detail in country-specific case studies in this chapter. Finally, the chapter will conclude with a discussion on the merits and challenges of attempting to quantify and index political risk.

The next section of this chapter will provide broader analysis and context for the results assigned to each state, including an update on consequential political events from 2016 and data provided from Freedom House. It should be noted that in the Freedom House "Freedom in the World" Report for 2016, the number of countries showing a decline in freedom for the year—72—was the largest since the 10-year slide began. Just 43 countries made gains.

The organization argues

the world was battered by crises that fueled xenophobic sentiment in democratic countries, undermined the economies of states dependent on the sale of natural resources, and led authoritarian regimes to crack down harder on dissent. These developments contributed to the 10th consecutive year of decline in global freedom.[3]

Armenia

Quick Facts—Armenia[4]	
Freedom Status: Partly Free	Capital: Yerevan
Aggregate Score: 46	Population: 3,017,106
Freedom Rating: 4.5	GDP/capita: $3,619.80
Political Rights: 5	Press Freedom: Not Free
Civil Liberties: 4	Net Freedom Status: Free

Corruption, constitutional reform, and a troubled geopolitical environment continued to present challenges to Armenia in 2015. In January of that year, Armenia became a member of the Eurasian Economic Union, a regional trade alliance with Russia, Belarus, Kazakhstan, and Kyrgyzstan, which joined later in the year.

In August, President Serzh Sargsyan formally submitted a reform proposal to transform Armenia's semipresidential government into a

---

[3] https://freedomhouse.org/report/freedom-world/freedom-world-2016

[4] https://freedomhouse.org/report/freedom-world/2016/armenia

parliamentary system with an empowered prime minister.[5] Armenia has a semipresidential system with a directly elected president who may serve two consecutive 5-year terms. The prime minister, nominated by a parliamentary majority and appointed by the president, forms the government. The legislature, the unicameral National Assembly, is made up of 131 members serving 5-year terms. Ninety seats are chosen by proportional representation, and 41 are decided through races in single-member districts.

The Republican Party of Armenia (HHK) and Sargsyan dominate political decision making.[6] The National Assembly includes some of the country's wealthiest business leaders, who continue entrepreneurial activities despite conflicts of interest. Relationships between politicians and other oligarchs also influence policy and contribute to selective application of the law.

As a result, corruption remains pervasive.[7] Some senior officials faced judicial and disciplinary action for corruption-related offenses in 2015, and the government overhauled and renewed funding for the Anticorruption Council in February that year. The rule of law does not often prevail in civil or criminal cases, and authorities apply the law selectively. Rumors that the judiciary suffers from corruption and systemic political pressure were supported by a 2013 report from the ombudsman's office, which noted a price list for bribing judges to avoid particular charges.[8]

Finally, Armenia is a source and, to a lesser extent, destination country for men, women, and children subjected to sex and labor trafficking. According to the U.S. State Department's 2015 *Trafficking in Persons Report,* the government complies with the minimum standards for the elimination of trafficking, and cooperates with antitrafficking NGOs.

---

[5] https://theguardian.com/world/2015/dec/07/armenia-vote-disputed-referendum-president-powers

[6] https://armenpress.am/eng/news/876258/hhk-n-qaxaqakan-dashti-orakarg-dzevavoroxn-e-serzh-sargsyani.html

[7] See for example, http://business-anti-corruption.com/country-profiles/armenia

[8] For more, see https://pf-armenia.org/sites/default/files/documents/files/PFA_Corruption_Report.pdf

Azerbaijan

Quick Facts—Azerbaijan[9]	
Freedom Status: Not Free	Capital: Baku
Aggregate Score: 16	Population: 9,651,000
Freedom Rating: 6.5	GDP/capita: $7,884.20
Political Rights: 7	Press Freedom: Not Free
Civil Liberties: 6	Net Freedom Status: Partly Free

Azerbaijan's political rights rating declined from 6 to 7 in 2015 due to an intensified crackdown on criticism and dissent, widespread rights violations in connection with the November 1 parliamentary elections, and serious violations of the right to a fair trial.[10]

Azerbaijan's constitution provides for a strong presidency, and the 125-member Milli Majlis (National Assembly) exercises little or no independence from the executive branch. The president and members of parliament serve 5-year terms, and a 2009 referendum eliminated presidential term limits.[11] In reality, elections since the early 1990s have been considered neither free nor fair by international observers. The 2013 presidential election saw incumbent Aliyev—who succeeded his father, Heydar Aliyev, in 2003—reelected to a controversial third term in office, in a vote marred by widespread irregularities and electoral fraud.[12]

Corruption is widespread, and wealth from the country's massive oil and gas exports creates ever-greater opportunities for graft. Because critical institutions, including the media and judiciary, are largely subservient to the president and ruling party, government officials are rarely held accountable for corruption.

[9] https://freedomhouse.org/report/freedom-world/2016/azerbaijan
[10] https://freedomhouse.org/report/freedom-world/2016/azerbaijan
[11] http://news.bbc.co.uk/2/hi/7949327.stm
[12] See http://reuters.com/article/us-azerbaijan-election-idUSBRE99812Z20131009 and https://theatlantic.com/international/archive/2013/07/how-azerbaijan-is-like-em-the-godfather-em/277717/

Freedom House reports that

In 2012, the president signed a series of legal amendments to allow companies' organizational structures and ownership to remain secret, significantly limiting journalists' ability to uncover corruption. Although public officials are nominally required to submit financial disclosure reports, disclosure procedures and compliance remain unclear, and the reports are not publicly accessible. In April 2015, the Extractive Industries Transparency Initiative (EITI), an international platform that promotes good governance and transparency in resource-rich countries, demoted Azerbaijan from its membership to candidate status due to noncompliance with EITI standards for human rights.[13]

Belarus

Quick Facts—Belarus[14]	
Freedom Status: Not Free	Capital: Minsk
Aggregate Score: 17	Population: 9,524,247
Freedom Rating: 7	GDP/capita: $8,040
Political Rights: 6	Press Freedom: Not Free
Civil Liberties: 6.5	Net Freedom Status: Not Free

President Alyaksandr Lukashenka secured a fifth term in the October 2015 presidential election, which failed to meet international standards, according to observers from the Organization for Security and Cooperation in Europe (OSCE).[15] The president is elected for 5-year terms without limits. The 110 members of the Chamber of Representatives, the lower house of the rubber-stamp National Assembly, are popularly elected for 4 years from single-mandate constituencies. The upper chamber, the

---

[13] https://freedomhouse.org/report/freedom-world/2016/azerbaijan. See also http://business-anti-corruption.com/country-profiles/azerbaijan

[14] https://freedomhouse.org/report/freedom-world/2016/belarus

[15] http://telegraph.co.uk/news/worldnews/europe/belarus/11925324/Alexander-Lukashenko-The-leader-who-wants-to-turn-Belarus-into-a-North-Korean-style-dynasty.html

Council of the Republic, consists of 64 members serving 4-year terms; 56 are elected by regional councils, and 8 are appointed by the president.

Since Lukashenka was democratically elected to his first term in 1994, elections and referendums in Belarus have been marred by serious and systemic irregularities. The state controls 70 percent of the Belarusian economy, feeding widespread corruption. In addition, graft is encouraged by an overall lack of transparency and accountability in government. Information on the work of about 60 government ministries and state-controlled companies, including the Ministry of Information and the state broadcaster, is classified. Belarus ranks 107 out of 168 countries and territories surveyed in Transparency International's 2015 Corruption Perceptions Index.[16]

The war in neighboring Ukraine, growing regional tensions, and a failing economy motivated Belarus to seek better relations with Europe and the United States during the year. In February, Lukashenka hosted leaders of France, Germany, Russia, and Ukraine for talks that resulted in a new ceasefire agreement[17] and in late October 2015, the government was rewarded for the steps it had taken to improve its still-repressive human rights situation when the European Union and the United States granted the country temporary relief from sanctions.[18]

Most recently, tensions with Russia heightened after Russia moved to secure the previously open border shared between the two states. At his February 2017 press conference, President Lukashenka said Russia had "crossed out" existing treaties with Belarus "with the stroke of a pen."[19] The Belarusian president also accused Russia of trying to bolster its influence over Belarus by pushing to control its energy pipelines and using oil and gas supplies as a lever of power.[20] At the same press conference,

---

[16] https://transparency.org/country/BLR

[17] https://nytimes.com/2015/02/12/world/europe/meeting-of-world-leaders-in-belarus-aims-to-address-ukraine-conflict.html?_r=0

[18] http://europarl.europa.eu/RegData/etudes/BRIE/2017/595878/EPRS_BRI(2017)595878_EN.pdf

[19] http://rferl.org/a/belarus-lukashenka-chaos-and-conflict-press-conference/28276919.html

[20] http://rferl.org/a/belarus-lukashenka-chaos-and-conflict-press-conference/28276919.html

the president stated unequivocally that Belarus does not plan to quit the Eurasian Economic Union, of which Russia, Belarus, Armenia, Kazakhstan, and Kyrgyzstan are members.

Georgia

Quick Facts—Georgia[21]	
Freedom Status: Partly Free	Capital: Tbilisi
Aggregate Score: 64	Population: 4,000,000
Freedom Rating: 3	GDP/capita: $3,796
Political Rights: 3	Press Freedom: Partly Free
Civil Liberties: 3	Net Freedom Status: Free

Freedom House analysts argue that democratic institutions and practices in Georgia saw signs of development, stagnation, and even regression in 2015. Positively, the year saw increased evidence of political pluralism and a noticeable slowing in new prosecutions against former officials from the previously ruling United National Movement (UNM), while the structural independence and functionality of the Georgian judicial system were largely sustained in 2015.[22] For the most part, the year was characterized by relative political stability. The intensity of partisan rancor between the ruling Georgian Dream (GD) and the opposition UNM was somewhat less apparent during the year, likely due in part to the absence of high-profile election events.

Ambiguity over shared power between the presidency and premiership did put Prime Minister Gharibashvili and President Giorgi Margvelashvili increasingly at odds in 2014 and 2015.[23] In 2014, Gharibashvili and Margvelashvili fought over attendance at the United Nations (UN) Climate

---

[21] https://freedomhouse.org/report/freedom-world/2017/georgia

[22] https://freedomhouse.org/report/nations-transit/2016/georgia

[23] "Georgian Prime Minister Acknowledges 'Worsened' Ties with President," Radio Free Europe/Radio Liberty (RFE/RL), September 15, 2014, http://rferl.org/content/garibashvili-margvelashvili-un-ties-worsening-problem-visit-statement/26584943.html

Summit,[24] and in September 2015, the two leaders sparred again over representation at the UN General Assembly.[25] Margvelashvili, preempted from a UN appearance by Gharibashvili, took a separate trip to the United States in the same period, and complained publicly that the Georgian Ambassador to the United States, who accompanied the prime minister at the UN, showed insufficient deference to the presidential office.[26]

Recent polls indicate that some segments of the Georgian public increasingly embrace pro-Russian and anti-Western policies,[27] though they continue to represent the minority and their support significantly lags behind that of Euro-Atlantic integration. Pro-Russian political parties in Georgia are widely seen as being funded by Moscow and part of Russia's efforts to extend its influence over Georgia and destabilize the country.[28]

Kazakhstan

Quick Facts—Kazakhstan[29]	
Freedom Status: Not Free	Capital: Astana
Aggregate Score: 22	Population: 17,800,000
Freedom Rating: 6	GDP/capita: $10,510
Political Rights: 7	Press Freedom: Not Free
Civil Liberties: 5	Net Freedom Status: Not Free

---

[24] "President and PM at Odds over UN Visit, Again," Civil Georgia, August 19, 2015, http://civil.ge/eng/article.php?id=28509

[25] "With His UN Visit 'Thwarted,' President Responds to Critics, Lays Out His Role," Civil Georgia, September 11, 2014, http://civil.ge/eng/article.php?id=27658

[26] "Georgian President Criticized Ambassador to the US," Georgia Today, October 6, 2015, http://georgiatoday.ge/news/1457/Georgian-President-Criticized-Ambassador-to-the-US

[27] Thornton, L., and D. Sichinava. 2015. "Public Attitudes in Georgia: Results of a April 2015 Survey Carried Out for NDI by CRRC Georgia." National Democratic Institute (NDI), May11, https://ndi.org/files/NDI percent20Georgia_April percent202015 percent20Poll_Public percent20Issues_ENG_VF_0.pdf

[28] Edilashvili, M. 2014. "Moscow Calling?," Transitions Online, July15, http://tol.org/client/article/24385-moscow-calling.html

[29] https://freedomhouse.org/report/freedom-world/2017/kazakhstan

Freedom House analysts believe that Kazakhstan's political rights rating declined from 6 to 7 in 2017 due to voters' lack of access to any genuine political choice and the continuation of efforts by the government to stifle opportunities for opposition groups. In April 2015, Nursultan Nazarbayev won a landslide victory in an early presidential election, securing a fifth term in office.[30] Government corruption and the president's family remained taboo subjects in the press, social media, and academia, and official hostility toward discussion of two additional controversial topics, the conflict in Ukraine and the spread of the Islamic State (IS) militant group in Central Asia, further diminished space for freedom of expression. Authorities also continued imposing restrictions on freedoms of assembly and association during the year.[31]

Kazakhstan became a member of the World Trade Organization (WTO) in June. New criminal, criminal executive, and administrative codes, however, went into effect in January and contained wide restrictions on the formation and operation of NGOs, including enhanced penalties for the leaders of organizations as well as general restrictions on activities not sanctioned by their organizations' charters.[32] The legislation also contained restrictions on the ability of individuals to organize and hold public gatherings. Foreign citizens cannot create public associations, but can become members.

Kyrgyzstan

Quick Facts—Kyrgyzstan[33]	
Freedom Status: Partly Free	Capital: Bishkek
Aggregate Score: 37	Population: 6,100,000
Freedom Rating: 5	GDP/capita: $1,103
Political Rights: 5	Press Freedom: Not Free
Civil Liberties: 5	Net Freedom Status: Partly Free

In March 2015, Prime Minister Joomart Otorbayev and his government resigned[34] after failing to negotiate a more advantageous agreement with

---

[30] https://nytimes.com/2015/04/28/world/asia/nursultan-a-nazarbayev-kazakh-stan-re-elected.html

[31] https://monitor.civicus.org/country/kazakhstan/

[32] http://icnl.org/research/monitor/kazakhstan.html

[33] https://freedomhouse.org/report/freedom-world/2016/kyrgyzstan

[34] http://rferl.org/a/kyrgyzstan-atambaev-otorbaev-resignation/26976544.html

the country's largest foreign investor, the Canadian mining firm Centerra Gold. The parliament confirmed Temir Sariyev as the new prime minister in May.[35] He is a long-serving politician who is widely regarded as having close ties to Russia, which became even more significant as Kyrgyzstan officially joined the Russian-led Eurasian Economic Union in August.[36]

Throughout 2015, nationalist and vigilante groups intensified harassment of minority populations that are perceived to be favored by Western countries.[37] European and U.S. organizations faced similar intimidation as well as legal pressure.[38] Although legislation modeled on Russia's "foreign agents" law continued to enjoy public support from President Almazbek Atambayev, it had yet to be adopted at the end of 2015.[39]

Kyrgyzstan was ranked 123 out of 168 countries and territories surveyed in Transparency International's 2015 Corruption Perceptions Index. An opinion survey conducted in early 2015 by the International Republican Institute found that 42 percent of Kyrgyzstanis believe that their parliament is "very corrupt," and another 37 percent consider it "somewhat corrupt."[40]

Moldova

Quick Facts—Moldova[41]	
Freedom Status: Partly Free	Capital: Chisinau
Aggregate Score: 62	Population: 3,600,00
Freedom Rating: 3	GDP/capita: $1,848
Political Rights: 3	Press Freedom: Partly Free
Civil Liberties: 3	Net Freedom Status: Partly Free

---

[35] http://thediplomat.com/2016/04/kyrgyzstan-gets-new-prime-minister-and-speaker/

[36] http://rferl.org/a/kyrgyzstan-eurasian-economic-union/27184629.html

[37] http://lse.ac.uk/internationaldevelopment/research/crisisstates/download/wp/wpseries2/wp792.pdf

[38] http://tribunecontentagency.com/article/european-environmental-team-harassed-in-kyrgyzstan/

[39] http://eurasianet.org/node/73721

[40] https://transparency.org/country/KGZ

[41] https://freedomhouse.org/report/freedom-world/2017/russia

Moldova experienced a significant political crisis in 2015,[42] as the aftershock of a banking scandal[43] and discord among parliamentary parties and prominent officials caused deep government dysfunction and stalled ongoing reform efforts.[44] Details about a major fraud scheme involving three Moldovan banks continued to emerge during the year, implicating high-ranking public figures and leading to mass protests. According to Freedom House, "the tense climate complicated the process of government formation, contributing to disagreements among the parties that had won seats in the November 2014 parliamentary elections."[45] After multiple transfers of power, the year ended in a political impasse, with parties unable to form a new governing coalition.

The banking scandal, in particular, emphasized the depth of influence wielded by the country's business elites on the political process, and underlined the extent of corruption at all levels of government. The scandal had serious financial consequences for the country, contributing to the devaluation of the leu, inflation, and the suspension of assistance from the International Monetary Fund (IMF), World Bank, and EU. Moldova was ranked 103 out of 168 countries and territories surveyed in Transparency International's 2015 Corruption Perceptions Index.[46]

Russia

Quick Facts—Russia[47]	
Freedom Status: Not Free	Capital: Moscow
Aggregate Score: 20	Population: 144,300,00
Freedom Rating: 6.5	GDP/capita: $9,093
Political Rights: 7	Press Freedom: Not Free
Civil Liberties: 7	Net Freedom Status: Not Free

---

[42] http://bbc.com/news/world-europe-35366194

[43] https://forbes.com/sites/kenrapoza/2016/08/01/billion-dollar-theft-in-moldova-one-rich-bankers-crime-has-a-nation-doing-time/#5079100d4f7e

[44] https://eeas.europa.eu/sites/eeas/files/joint_analysis_0.pdf

[45] https://freedomhouse.org/report/freedom-world/2016/moldova

[46] http://transparency.org/news/pressrelease/corruption_index_reflects_moldovas_disappointing_response_to_corruption

[47] https://freedomhouse.org/report/freedom-world/2017/russia

According to Freedom House analysts, Russia's economy continued to deteriorate in 2015 as "the Kremlin worked to preempt potential domestic discontent through the distraction of foreign interventions."[48] With the conflict in eastern Ukraine settling into a stalemate, President Vladimir Putin sent Russian aircraft to Syria in September[49] and began bombing the opponents of Syrian leader Bashar al-Assad, directly engaging the Russian military outside the former Soviet Union for the first time since Soviet troops left Afghanistan.[50]

Domestically, the Kremlin continued a crackdown on civil society, ramping up pressure on domestic nongovernmental organizations (NGOs) and branding the United States-based National Endowment for Democracy and two groups backed by billionaire philanthropist George Soros as "undesirable organizations."[51] Freedom House also reported that the regime "intensified its tight grip on the media, saturating the information landscape with nationalist propaganda while suppressing the most popular alternative voices. In the annual round of regional and local elections, serious opposition candidates were again prevented from competing."[52]

The economy shrank by approximately 4 percent over the course of the year due to structural problems,[53] falling oil prices,[54] Ukraine-related sanctions,[55] and the Kremlin's own countersanctions on European imports.[56] In another sign that the country's aggressive foreign policy was

---

[48] https://freedomhouse.org/report/freedom-world/2016/russia

[49] http://bbc.com/news/world-middle-east-34416519

[50] https://freedomhouse.org/report/freedom-world/2016/russia

[51] http://washingtontimes.com/news/2015/nov/30/pro-democracy-groups-funded-billionaire-soros-bann/ and https://nytimes.com/2016/03/12/world/europe/national-democratic-institute-banned-russia.html

[52] https://freedomhouse.org/report/freedom-world/2016/russia

[53] https://osw.waw.pl/sites/default/files/raport_crisis_in_russia_net.pdf

[54] Tatiana, M. 2016. *Shifting Political Economy of Russian Oil and Gas, Center for Strategic International Studies*, p. 3.

[55] http://reuters.com/article/us-ukraine-crisis-russia-minerals-idUSBRE-A3N1EK20140424

[56] http://carnegie.ru/2017/02/02/decline-not-collapse-bleak-prospects-for-russia-s-economy-pub-67865

increasing its international isolation, the government imposed new sanctions on a variety of Turkish goods and companies after a Turkish fighter jet shot down a Russian warplane over Syria in November.[57]

In some cases, analysts note that the Kremlin appeared to signal to officials that corruption needed to be scaled down given Russia's growing economic difficulties. Vladimir Yakunin, a powerful member of Putin's inner circle, resigned under pressure as head of Russian Railways in August,[58] with some reports saying that corruption was a factor. Freedom House reports argue that the move was "seen as significant because control over key state companies provides favored individuals with access to considerable funds."[59]

Tajikistan

Quick Facts—Tajikistan[60]	
Freedom Status: Not Free	Capital: Dushanbe
Aggregate Score: 11	Population: 8,600,00
Freedom Rating: 6.5	GDP/capita: $926
Political Rights: 7	Press Freedom: Not Free
Civil Liberties: 6	Net Freedom Status: Not Free

According to recent reports, Tajikistani authorities continued to "arbitrarily limit free speech, access to information, and the right to civic organization in 2015."[61] The government led a legal and media campaign against the country's largest opposition group, the Islamic Renaissance Party of Tajikistan (IRPT), ahead of and following parliamentary elections in March,[62] in which the ruling People's Democratic Party (PDP) retained its majority. In September, after a series of decisions revoking the

---

[57] http://money.cnn.com/2015/11/30/news/economy/russia-turkey-plane-sanctions/

[58] http://uk.reuters.com/article/uk-rzd-yakunin-idUKKCN0QN0TY20150818

[59] https://freedomhouse.org/report/freedom-world/2016/russia

[60] https://freedomhouse.org/report/freedom-world/2017/tajikistan

[61] https://freedomhouse.org/report/freedom-world/2016/tajikistan

[62] https://hrw.org/news/2016/02/17/tajikistan-severe-crackdown-political-opposition

legal status of the IRPT and limiting its activities, the Supreme Court declared the party a terrorist organization, criminalizing membership in or public expression of support for the group.[63] Authorities shuttered IRPT offices and arrested scores of members following the decision.

Patronage networks and regional affiliations are central to political life, and corruption is pervasive. Major irregularities at the National Bank of Tajikistan[64] and the country's largest industrial company, TALCO Aluminum,[65] have been documented and linked together. Tajikistan was ranked 136 out of 168 countries and territories surveyed in Transparency International's 2015 Corruption Perceptions Index.[66] Public officials are not required to disclose financial information, and government decision making and budgetary processes lack transparency.

Turkmenistan

Quick Facts—Turkmenistan[67]	
Freedom Status: Not Free	Capital: Ashgabat
Aggregate Score: 3	Population: 5,400,00
Freedom Rating: 7	GDP/capita: $6,672
Political Rights: 7	Press Freedom: Not Free
Civil Liberties: 7	Net Freedom Status: Not Free

Analysts from Freedom House argue that President Gurbanguly Berdymukhammedov's government reinforced its repressive controls on politics and society in 2015.[68] During the year, "legislators discussed constitutional changes that would allow the president to serve for an unlimited number of terms. State authorities continued to limit the availability

---

[63] http://rferl.org/a/tajikistan-islamic-party-members-trial-begins/27541023.html

[64] http://rferl.org/a/Tajik_Audit_Reveals_Huge_National_Bank_Shortfalls/1609233.html

[65] http://eurasianet.org/node/68466

[66] https://transparency.org/country/TJK

[67] https://freedomhouse.org/report/freedom-world/2017/turkmenistan

[68] http://civicus.org/index.php/media-resources/media-releases/2735-turkmenistan-s-elections-under-cloud-as-civil-society-faces-total-clampdown

of independent information, harass and imprison critics, and pressure ethnic and religious minorities."[69] International criticism and pressure have not led to genuine respect for fundamental freedoms by the government. When confronted with accusations of human rights violations at the annual Human Dimension Implementation Meeting hosted by the OSCE in September, the delegation from Turkmenistan denied the claims, calling them "subjective, provocative attacks and biased comments."[70]

Corruption in Turkmenistan, which was ranked 154 out of 168 countries and territories surveyed in Transparency International's 2015 Corruption Perceptions Index, is widespread.[71] Many public officials are widely understood to have bribed their way into their positions. The government's lack of transparency affects nearly all spheres of the economy and public services.

Ukraine

Quick Facts—Ukraine[72]	
Freedom Status: Partly Free	Capital: Kyiv
Aggregate Score: 61	Population: 42,700,00
Freedom Rating: 3	GDP/capita: $2,115
Political Rights: 3	Press Freedom: Partly Free
Civil Liberties: 3	Net Freedom Status: Partly Free

According to most analysts, conditions in Ukraine stabilized somewhat in 2015 compared with the previous year, which included the Euromaidan protests,[73] the downfall of President Viktor Yanukovych,[74] Russia's occupation of Crimea and invasion of the Donbas,[75] and presidential and parliamentary elections. With Crimea still held by Russia and continued fighting between government forces and Russian-backed separatists in

---

[69] https://freedomhouse.org/report/freedom-world/2016/turkmenistan

[70] http://osce.org/odihr/hdim_2016

[71] https://transparency.org/country/TKM

[72] https://freedomhouse.org/report/freedom-world/2017/ukraine

[73] http://euromaidanpress.com/2016/02/20/the-story-of-ukraine-starting-from-euromaidan/2/

[74] http://bbc.com/news/world-europe-25182830

[75] http://worldaffairsjournal.org/article/ukraine-invasion-one-year-later

eastern Ukraine, President Petro Poroshenko's top priority was restoring the country's territorial integrity and peace within its borders.[76] The leaders of Ukraine, Russia, France, and Germany agreed in February to the so-called Minsk II accord, which called for a cease-fire, withdrawal of heavy weapons from the front, release of hostages and detainees, changes in the Ukrainian constitution to give more autonomy to the regions, legislation on special status for parts of the Donbas regions of Donetsk and Luhansk, withdrawal of foreign forces from Ukraine, and restored Ukrainian government control over the eastern border by the end of 2015.[77]

Meanwhile, Ukraine continued to pursue greater integration with Europe. A free-trade agreement with the European Union (EU) was set to take effect at the beginning of 2016,[78] and much of Ukraine's previous trade with Russia has been cut off by tit-for-tat sanctions between the two countries.[79] However, obstacles to further integration include stalled anticorruption reforms and the activities of armed militia groups.

A package of anticorruption legislation adopted in 2014 is being implemented slowly. The reforms set up a National Anticorruption Bureau (NABU) to investigate corrupt officials, called for a National Agency for Corruption Prevention (NACP), and sought to establish a separate anticorruption section within the prosecutor general's office.[80]

Uzbekistan

Quick Facts—Uzbekistan[81]	
Freedom Status: Not Free	Capital: Tashkent
Aggregate Score: 3	Population: 31,900,000
Freedom Rating: 7	GDP/capita: $2,132
Political Rights: 7	Press Freedom: Not Free
Civil Liberties: 7	Net Freedom Status: Not Free

[76] http://president.gov.ua/en/news/vistup-prezidenta-ukrayini-na-zagalnih-debatah-70-yi-sesiyi-36057

[77] https://nytimes.com/2015/02/13/world/europe/ukraine-talks-cease-fire.html

[78] http://trade.ec.europa.eu/doclib/press/index.cfm?id=1425

[79] https://ft.com/content/bf171902-a41e-11e5-873f-68411a84f346

[80] https://nabu.gov.ua/en

[81] https://freedomhouse.org/report/freedom-world/2017/uzbekistan

In March 2015, President Islam Karimov was reelected to a fourth term with a reported 90 percent of the vote despite a constitutional limit of two consecutive terms.[82] The government continued to suppress all political opposition during the year. The few remaining civic activists and critical journalists in the country faced physical violence, prosecution, hefty fines, involuntary hospitalization, and arbitrary detention. In an exceptional case in February, authorities released popular journalist and religious figure Hayrullo Hamidov, who served 5 years of a 6-year sentence on religious extremism charges.[83]

Gulnara Karimova, the president's elder daughter, remained under house arrest in 2015 amid persisting allegations of corruption and links to organized crime.[84] Several high-ranking officials who played a role in the case against Karimova and her associates were dismissed, signaling what many analysts believe are ongoing shifts in internal competition for power and resources.

Corruption is pervasive. Uzbekistan was ranked 153 out of 168 countries and territories surveyed in Transparency International's 2015 Corruption Perceptions Index.[85] Graft and bribery among low- and mid-level officials are common and at times even transparent. Social-media platforms have given space to new public discourse on corruption, allowing citizens to self-document bribery and other malfeasance. Citizens have made efforts to gather and publicize evidence of abuse of office in some sectors, but these attempts have not been successful in compelling the government to change Uzbekistan's entrenched culture of corruption.

Assessing Political Risk

As barriers to regional and international trade are lowered, investors continue to seek new opportunities in emerging markets around the world.

---

[82] https://theguardian.com/world/2015/mar/30/islam-karimov-re-elected-uzbekistans-president-in-predicted-landslide

[83] https://cpj.org/2017/02/

[84] https://theguardian.com/world/2014/sep/16/uzbekistan-first-daughter-gulnara-karimova-house-arrest

[85] https://transparency.org/cpi2015/

As we have seen in the individual case studies, these markets are vulnerable to a wide range of forces, known as political risk, which are beyond the control of potential investors. These risks might include corruption, unstable government institutions, reforming financial systems, uncertain legal systems or regulatory regimes, and even currency instability.

Techniques for assessing these risks are wide ranging, from traditional methods employing comparative ratings and mapping systems (as illustrated in the case studies of this chapter), to special reports, expert systems, modeling, and logit analysis. No assessment method is perfect, and correlating the individual variables does not often yield accurate measurements of potential loss generated by political risk.

Yet, companies acknowledge that no matter their size, they must consider the political environment when planning to conduct business abroad. As noted in previous publications within this series, "one of the most undeniable and crucial realities of international business is that both host and home government are integral partners."[86]

Further, it is important to recognize that political risk is taking new and different forms in both advanced and emerging economies. This includes dealing with real or perceived income inequality, sovereign debt, state actions to promote state-owned companies, erecting of trade barriers—all of which have the potential pose serious threats to companies.

Businesses increasingly focus their attention on financial, market, and operational forms of risk, particularly in the wake of the 2008 economic crisis. According to a recent Global Risk Management study, most companies neither measure nor manage political risk. Instead, they tend to accept (or ignore) them, or avoid entering situations that post significant risk, even when they might lead to a significant opportunity for growth.[87]

Conclusion

Whether corporations and investors are conducting business abroad or investing in emerging markets, they are consistently exposed to political environments that atypical of advanced economies. The risk of major

---

[86] Goncalves et al. (2014).
[87] Deloitte (2012).

violence is greatest when states lack territorial integrity, recognized sovereignty, institutional legitimacy, or bureaucratic effectiveness and transparency. This vulnerability becomes increasingly apparent with the rise of unemployment, growing income inequality, public witnessing of corruption, and the development of alternative economies (blackmarkets, trafficking networks, etc.) within and across states.

There are many practical strategies that companies and investors can adopt to mitigate the impact of political risk.[88] In addition to the factors discussed in Prof. Marcus Goncalves' recent publication (cited in the following), he also suggests working with one of a few great companies, such as ACE Global Markets,[89] that cover emerging market risks and focus on three specific areas: political insurance, trade credit, and trade credit insurance. Political risk insurance covers investments and trade by addressing issues related to the confiscation of assets and interruption of trade. They can also assist with managing structured trade credit, short and medium term, and extending trade credit insurance.

---

[88] See Marcus Goncalves, "Coping with Political and Economic Risks," in Doing Business in Emerging Markets: Roadmap for Success, Edition: 1st, Chapter: 3, Publisher: Business Expert Press, Editors: Philip J. Romero, Jeffrey A. Edwards, p. 31

[89] www.aceglobalmarkets.com

CHAPTER 6

Future Considerations and Challenges to Growth

Overview

Belarus President Alexander Lukashenko extended a warm message to the leaders of the Commonwealth of Independent States (CIS) member states on the occasion of the 25th anniversary of the CIS. The head of state noted that the CIS Treaty which was signed on December 8, 1991 marked the start of integration in the post-Soviet space. "Over the past 25 years, relying on the principles of respect for national priorities and freedom of expression of its member states, the CIS has grown into a modern regional community that considers the interests of all the parties," Lukashenko stressed.

The president emphasized a renewed commitment in 2016 to adapt the CIS to the present-day challenges and confirmed that he is confident that this landmark event will strengthen the image of the CIS, making it an even more relevant organization. Despite major differences country-to-country, groups within each state share many common economic, political, and cultural characteristics, which many hope will fade with the passing of those generations that remember the common state. In this context, the Russian Federation holds a unique position in the Euro-Pacific area. Separate, distinct, but still bordering these regions and related to all of them to differing degrees, in the 2010s Russia will step up efforts to become an independent center of gravity in Northern Eurasia. Leaning on its CIS allies and partners, Moscow is willing to fortify its stance vis-à-vis its geopolitical competitors—the European Union in the west, and China in the east.

Russia and the CIS continue to experience appreciable slack. Output gaps remain negative, on the back of subdued private consumption and investment, and real credit growth, while improving, is still negative. Although still elevated, inflation in these countries has declined, reflecting the still negative output gaps together with lower-than-expected exchange rate pass through and declining international food prices.

The decline in foreign banks' claims on CIS countries accelerated after these countries slipped into recession in 2014. Since late 2015, however, external positions of the Bank for International Settlements (BIS)-reporting banks outside the CIS have shown some signs of stabilization. According to bank surveys, Western banks adjusted their exposures in the region, differentiating across countries based on their economic prospects and progress on private nonfinancial sector deleveraging. Banks have gradually increased exposures to countries with better economic fundamentals and market potential, while continuing to withdraw from countries struggling with high nonperformance loans, high corporate leverage, and weak aggregate demand. Going forward, challenges remain, as many European banks continue to struggle with still high levels of impaired assets and low profitability in a low-growth and low-interest rate environment (IMF 2016, Chapter 1).

In Russia, following a significant moderation of the recession in 2016, GDP is projected to return to growth in 2017 supported by higher oil prices. In the CIS, the recovery is projected to gather pace in 2017, supported by an improved outlook in Russia, given the close linkages between Russia and the rest of the CIS through trade and remittances. Inflation is projected to moderate further over the near term reflecting somewhat stronger exchange rates.

Prospects for 2017

This book had provided a regional analysis, as well as country scan (see Appendix A), of the CIS regional block economies. We examined their history since the breakup of the formal Soviet Union and the formation of the CIS bloc, including creation of regional agreements such as the CIS Free Trade Area and the Eurasian Economic Union, a single economic market which now represents more than 180 million people.

What lies ahead in coordinating this economic, political, and security collective? Most analysts are predicting a gradual improvement in the region's economic backdrop in 2017, as the easing of geopolitical tensions and the expected recovery in commodity prices will support faster growth in the CIS this year. Acknowledging the state's significant influence over the politics and economies of the CIS region, they are basing their predictions of improvement on an expectation of return to growth in Russia. More broadly, strengthening economic activity in Azerbaijan, Kazakhstan, and Russia will support growth in the subregions of Central Asia and the Caucasus.

Nevertheless, the combination of factors that determined the plunge in the economy of the CIS since the second quarter of 2015 still persists today. These factors included the sharp fall in commodities prices, restrictions on access to international capital markets due to sanctions against Russia and a deceleration in China, which is the region's main trading partner. Although economic conditions in most of the CIS economies are challenging, differences in growth dynamics persist. Oil and gas exporting countries, namely Azerbaijan, Kazakhstan, Russia and Turkmenistan, are seeing economic conditions deteriorating rapidly because of the sharp fall in energy prices. Meanwhile, most of the labor-exporting countries (Armenia, Kyrgyzstan, Moldova, and Tajikistan) are seeing the deterioration in growth rates, mainly due to strong production in the agricultural sector and, in some cases, increased activity in the extractive sector.

APPENDIX A

Country Scanning of the CIS States

The following is a brief scanning of the Commonwealth of Independent States (CIS) countries to help in the understanding of their challenges and competitive advantages in furthering their economies and global market integrations that are discussed in this book. The CIS is a regional organization which was created in December 1991 by the former Soviet Republics. In the adopted *Declaration,* the participants of the *Commonwealth* declared their interaction based on sovereign equality.

Originally, there were 12 member states that were part of the CIS, including Azerbaijan, Armenia, Belarus, Kazakhstan, Kyrgyzstan, Moldova, Russia, Tajikistan, Turkmenistan, Uzbekistan, Ukraine, and Georgia. Both Ukraine and Georgia left the CIS in 2014 and 2009, respectively.

Armenia

Armenia is a unitary, multiparty, democratic nation-state with an ancient cultural heritage. The Satrapy of Armenia was established in the 6th century BC, after the fall of Urartu. In the 1st century BC the Kingdom of Armenia reached its height under Tigranes the Great. Armenia became the first country in the world to adopt Christianity as its official religion[1] in between late 3rd century to early years of the 4th century, becoming the first Christian nation.[2] Thus, previously predominant Zoroastrianism and paganism in Armenia gradually declined.

---

[1] Garsoïan, N. 1997. *Armenian People from Ancient to Modern Times.* Vol. 1, 81. Palgrave Macmillan.
[2] Stringer, M.D. 2005. *A Sociological History of Christian Worship,* 92. Cambridge: Cambridge University Press.

Figure A.1 *Armenia is bordered by Turkey to the west, Georgia to the north, the de facto independent Nagorno-Karabakh Republic and Azerbaijan to the east, and Iran and the Azerbaijani exclave of Nakhchivan to the south*

Source: Magellan Geographix.

As depicted in Figure A.1, Armenia is a landlocked country in the South Caucasus region of Eurasia, bordered by Turkey to the west, Georgia to the north, the de facto independent Nagorno-Karabakh Republic and Azerbaijan to the east, and Iran and the Azerbaijani exclave of Nakhchivan to the south. Armenia is the second most densely populated country of the former Soviet republics because of its small size.

Between the 16th century and first half of the 19th century, the traditional Armenian homeland composed of Eastern Armenia and Western Armenia came under rule of the rivaling Ottoman and successive Iranian Empires, passing between the two over the centuries. By the mid-19th century, Eastern Armenia had been conquered by Russia from Qajar Iran, while most of the western parts of the traditional Armenian homeland remained under Ottoman rule.

During World War I, the Armenians living in their ancestral lands in the Ottoman Empire were systematically exterminated in the Armenian Genocide in two phases: the wholesale killing of the able-bodied male population through massacre and subjection of army conscripts to forced labor, followed by the deportation of women, children, the elderly, and infirm on death marches leading to the Syrian desert. Driven forward by military escorts, the deportees were deprived of food and water and subjected to periodic robbery, rape, and massacre.[3, 4] The Armenian Genocide is acknowledged to have been one of the first modern genocides.[5] As per the research conducted by Arnold J. Toynbee, an estimated 600,000 Armenians died during deportation from 1915 to 1916. This figure, however, accounts for solely the first year of the Genocide and does not consider those who died or were killed after the report was compiled on the May 24, 1916.[6] The International Association of Genocide Scholars places the death toll at "more than a million."[7] The total number of people killed has been most widely estimated at between 1 and 1.5 million.[8]

In 1918, during the Russian Revolution, all non-Russian countries were granted independence from the dissolved empire, leading to the establishment of the First Republic of Armenia. By 1920, the state was incorporated into the Transcaucasian Socialist Federative Soviet Republic, a founding member of the Soviet Union in 1922. In 1936, the Transcaucasian state was dissolved, leaving its constituent states, including the Armenian Soviet Socialist Republic, as full Union republics. The modern Republic of Armenia became independent in 1991 during the dissolution of the Soviet Union.

---

[3] Kieser, H.L., and D.J. Schaller. 2002. Der Völkermord an den Armeniern und die Shoah [The Armenian genocide and the Shoah] (in German), Chronos, p. 114.

[4] Walker, C.J. 1980. *Armenia: The Survival of A Nation*, 200–3. London: Croom Helm.

[5] Ferguson, N. 2006. *The War of the World: Twentieth-Century Conflict and the Descent of the West*, 177. New York: Penguin Press.

[6] Robert, M. 1992. *Revolution and Genocide: On the Origins of the Armenian Genocide and the Holocaust*, 147. University of Chicago Press.

[7] BBC 2008. "Q&A: Armenian genocide dispute." BBC News, http://news.bbc.co.uk/2/hi/europe/6045182.stm, last accessed on 01/10/2016.

[8] Ibidem.

Until its independence, Armenia's economy was based largely on industries including chemicals, electronic products, machinery, processed food, synthetic rubber, and textiles. It has also been highly dependent on outside resources. Agriculture accounted for only 20 percent of net material product and 10 percent of employment before the breakup of the Soviet Union in 1991. Armenian mines produce copper, zinc, gold, and lead. The clear majority of energy is produced with imported fuel, including gas and nuclear fuel from Russia, to power its single nuclear power plant. The main domestic energy source is hydroelectric. Small amounts of coal, gas, and petroleum have not yet been developed.

Like other former states, Armenia's economy suffers from the legacy of a centrally planned economy and the breakdown of former Soviet trading patterns. Soviet investment in and support of Armenian industry has virtually disappeared, so that few major enterprises are still able to function. In addition, the effects of the 1988 earthquake, which killed more than 25,000 people and left more than 500,000 people homeless, are still being felt. Although a ceasefire has held since 1994, the conflict with Azerbaijan over Nagorno-Karabakh has not been resolved. The consequent blockade along both the Azerbaijani and Turkish borders has devastated the economy, because of Armenia's dependence on outside supplies of energy and most raw materials. Land routes through Azerbaijan and Turkey are still closed, while routes through Georgia and Iran are adequate and reliable.

In 1992 to 1993, the GDP had fallen nearly 60 percent from its 1989 level. The national currency, the dram, suffered hyperinflation for the first few years after its introduction in 1993. Nonetheless, Armenia has registered strong economic growth since 1995 and inflation has been negligible for the past several years. New sectors, such as precious stone processing, jewelry making and communication technology are flourishing. This steady economic progress has earned Armenia increasing support from international institutions. The government has made major strides toward joining the WTO, which it joined in 2003. The government also launched in 1994 an ambitious IMF-sponsored economic liberalization program that resulted in growth rates in 1995 to 2005.

Armenia also has managed to slash inflation, stabilize its currency, and privatize most small and medium-sized enterprises (SMEs). Armenia's unemployment rate, however, remains high, despite strong economic growth. Armenia is now a net energy exporter, although it does not have sufficient generating capacity to replace its nuclear power plant in Metsamor, which is under international pressure to close. The electricity distribution system was privatized in 2002.

The IMF, World Bank, and the European Bank for Reconstruction and Development (EBRD), as well as other international financial institutions and foreign countries have been extending considerable grants and loans to the country targeted at reducing the budget deficit, stabilizing the local currency; developing private businesses; energy; the agriculture, food processing, transportation, and health and education sectors; and ongoing rehabilitation work in the earthquake zone. Hence, Armenia's severe trade imbalance has been offset somewhat by international aid, remittances from Armenians working abroad, and foreign direct investment.

Per the World Bank, and depicted in Figure A.2, the GDP per capita in Armenia was last recorded at $7,763.39 in 2014, when adjusted by purchasing power parity (PPP). The GDP per Capita, in Armenia, when adjusted by PPP is equivalent to 44 percent of the world's average. GDP per capita PPP in Armenia averaged $4,464.91 from 1990 until 2014, reaching an all-time high of $7,763.39 in 2014 and a record low of $1,841.72 in 1993.

Continued progress will depend on the ability of the government to strengthen its macroeconomic management, including increasing revenue collection, improving the investment climate, and accelerating

ARMENIA GDP PER CAPTIA PPP

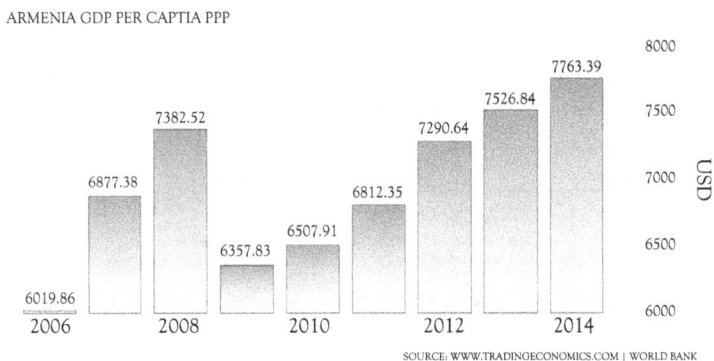

SOURCE: WWW.TRADINGECONOMICS.COM | WORLD BANK

Figure A.2 Armenia GDP per capita

Source: World Bank, tradingeconomics.com.

privatization. A liberal foreign investment law was approved in June 1994, and a law on privatization was adopted in 1997, as well as a program on state property privatization.

Azerbaijan

Located in the South Caucasus, Azerbaijan is a transcontinental country situated at the crossroads of The CIS and Western Asia. While often politically aligned with Europe, Azerbaijan is generally considered to be at least mostly in Southwest Asia geographically with its northern part bisected by the standard Asia-Europe divide, the Greater Caucasus. The UN and CIA classification of the country differs, with the UN placing Azerbaijan in Western Asia, while the CIA World Factbook places it mostly in Southwest Asia, and the Merriam-Webster's Collegiate Dictionary places them in both! We'll let you take a pick! Nonetheless, the country, as depicted in Figure A.3, bordered by the Caspian Sea to the east, Russia to the north, Georgia to the northwest, Armenia to the west and Iran to the south. In addition, the exclave of Nakhchivan is bounded by Armenia to the north and east, Iran to the south and west, while having a short border with Turkey in the northwest.

The country proclaimed its independence in 1918 and became the first Muslim-majority democratic and secular republic and to have operas, theaters and modern universities.[9,10] The Constitution of Azerbaijan does not declare an official religion, and all major political forces in the country are secularist, but most people and some opposition movements adhere to Shia Islam.[11] Azerbaijan was incorporated into the Soviet Union in 1920 as the Azerbaijan Soviet Socialist Republic, proclaiming its independence from the USSR in August 1991, before the official dissolution of the USSR.[12] In September 1991, the disputed Armenian-

---

[9] Tadeusz, S. 1995. *Russia and Azerbaijan: A Borderland in Transition*. New York, NY: Columbia University Press.

[10] Reinhard, S. 2000. *A Modern History of the Islamic World*. New York, NY: I.B. Tauris.

[11] Cornell, S.E. 2010. *Azerbaijan Since Independence*, 165, 284. North Castle, NY: M.E. Sharpe.

[12] King, D.C. 2006. *Azerbaijan*, 27. New York, NY: Cavendish Square Publishing.

Figure A.3 Azerbaijan is bordered by the Caspian Sea to the east, Russia to the north, and Georgia to the northwest, and Armenia to the west and Iran to the south

Source: CDC.

majority Nagorno-Karabakh region reaffirmed its willingness to create a separate state as the Nagorno-Karabakh Republic. The region, effectively independent since the beginning of the Nagorno-Karabakh War in 1991, is internationally recognized as part of Azerbaijan until a final solution to its status is found through negotiations facilitated by the Organization for Security and Cooperation in Europe (OSCE).[13]

Azerbaijan is a unitary semipresidential republic. The country is a member state of the Council of Europe, the OSCE and the NATO Partnership for Peace (PfP) program. It is one of the six independent Turkic-speaking states, being an active member of the Turkic Council and the TÜRKSOY community. The country has diplomatic relations with 158 countries and holds membership in 38 international organizations. It is one of the founding members of the CIS[14] and Organization for

---

[13] Ibidem.

[14] Europa Publications Limited 1998. *The CIS and the Commonwealth of Independent States*, 154. Routledge. ISBN 978-1-85743-058-5.

the Prohibition of Chemical Weapons. Also, a member of the UN since 1992, Azerbaijan was elected to membership in the newly established Human Rights Council by the United Nations General Assembly in May 2006. The country is also a member state of the Non-Aligned Movement, holds observer status in World Trade Organization and is a correspondent at the International Telecommunication Union.

Economically, Azerbaijan has completed its post-Soviet transition into a major oil-based economy from one where the state played the major role. Economic growth has been spurred by the exploration and development of oil and gas reserves, high levels of public expenditure, and substantial reforms to support a market-based economy. Despite robust growth, the economy of Azerbaijan remains largely dependent upon the extraction and production of fossil fuels. Today, however, the country is an oil-rich economy whose gross national income per capita has increased approximately tenfold since 2001.

As depicted in Figure A.4, Azerbaijan's GDP per capita in Azerbaijan was last recorded at $16,710.30 in 2014, when adjusted by PPP. The country's GDP per capita when adjusted by PPP is equivalent to 94 percent of the world's average. GDP per capita PPP in Azerbaijan averaged $8,777.13 from 1990 until 2014, reaching an all-time high of $16,710.30 in 2014 and a record low of $3,319.77 in 1995.[15] Such rates

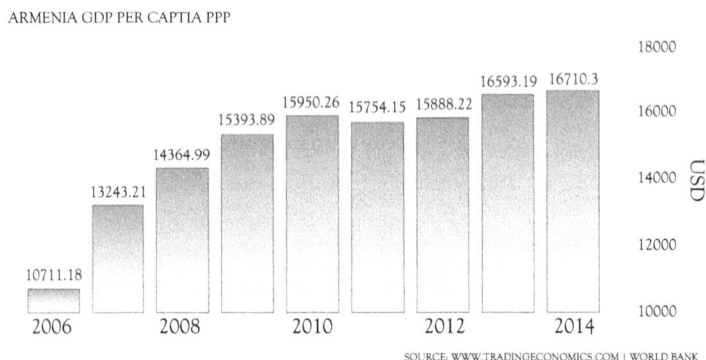

ARMENIA GDP PER CAPTIA PPP

SOURCE: WWW.TRADINGECONOMICS.COM | WORLD BANK

Figure A.4 Azerbaijan GDP growth

Source: World Bank, trendingeconomics.com.

---

[15] "RosBusinessConsulting—News Online." Rbcnews.com, http://rbcnews.com/free/20070403193147.shtml, last accessed on 01/10/2016.

cannot be sustained, but despite reaching 26.4 percent in 2005 (second highest GDP growth in the world in 2005 only to Equatorial Guinea), and 2006 over 34.6 percent (world highest), in 2008 dropped to 10.8 percent, and dropped further to 9.3 percent in 2009.[16] The national currency, the Azerbaijani manat, was stable in 2000, depreciating 3.8 percent against the dollar. The budget deficit equaled 1.3 percent of GDP in 2000.

Progress on economic reform has generally lagged macroeconomic stabilization. The government has undertaken regulatory reforms in some areas, including substantial opening of trade policy, but inefficient public administration in which commercial and regulatory interests are comingled limit the impact of these reforms. The government has largely completed privatization of agricultural lands and SMEs. In August 2000, the government launched a second-stage privatization program, in which many large state enterprises will be privatized. Since 2001, the economic activity in the country is regulated by the Ministry of Economic Development of Azerbaijan Republic.

The manat tumbled by more than 30 percent following Azerbaijan's switch from a currency peg to a free-floating exchange rate. The move, which represented the second drastic devaluation of the currency in 2015, is aimed at protecting the country's dwindling foreign exchange reserves, which have come under pressure from falling oil prices and the economic crisis in Russia, and to restore export competitiveness. Oil and gas account for more than 90 percent of Azerbaijan's exports and 70 percent of government revenues. While the devaluation seemed inevitable against the backdrop of tumbling foreign reserves, it will likely have a negative impact on salaries, pensions and savings in local currency, fuel inflation and increase concerns over the Azerbaijani banking sector, which has a large share of bank deposits denominated in foreign currency.

In 2015, Azerbaijan's economy rebounded, however, with robust growth of 5.7 percent in the first half of the year, up from 2.1 percent in the same period in 2014. Boosted mainly by government capital expenditure, the economy outside of the large petroleum sector was the major driver of growth. The public investment program remains a key source

---

[16] Today.Az—GDP growth makes 3.4 percent in Azerbaijan in 2009, http:// today.az/news/business/51114.html, last accessed on 01/12/2016.

of economic expansion and employment, but budget revenues are under pressure from lower oil prices.

Official foreign currency reserves fell by more than 30 percent in January to August 2015 because the central bank intervened to maintain the new exchange rate after the February 2015 devaluation of the Azerbaijan manat. Oil prices, key to local currency stability, have fallen dramatically over the past year, from $103.08 per barrel of Azeri light crude in August 2014 to $46.23 a year later.

To limit inflation, the central bank has reduced local currency liquidity. With tepid domestic demand, largely offsetting price pressures from the devaluation, year-on-year inflation rose to only 3.5 percent in the first half of 2015, which was nevertheless up from 1.6 percent for the same period in 2014. The devaluation will continue to put inflationary pressure on imports other than food.

Azerbaijan faces a multifaceted crisis in 2016 to 2017. Low oil prices led to a major currency devaluation in 2015, which will depress consumption and investment and push up inflation. Pressure on the currency remains high, and the authorities imposed currency controls in mid-January 2016. The banking sector will suffer major losses this year, and depend heavily on state support. Falling incomes and rising unemployment will lead to protests in some areas and a rise in political uncertainty.

Belarus

Belarus, as depicted in Figure A.5, is a landlocked country in the CIS bordered by Russia to the northeast, Ukraine to the south, Poland to the west, and Lithuania and Latvia to the northwest. Its capital is Minsk, and count with over 40 percent of its 207,600 square kilometers (80,200 sq. mi.) is forested. Its strongest economic sectors are service industries and manufacturing.

Until the 20th century, different states at various times controlled the lands of today's Belarus. In the aftermath of the 1917 Russian Revolution, Belarus declared independence as the Belarusian People's Republic, succeeded by the Socialist Soviet Republic of Byelorussia, which became a founding constituent republic of the Soviet Union in 1922, then renamed as the Byelorussian Soviet Socialist Republic. The country lost almost half

Figure A.5 Belarus is a landlocked country in the CIS bordered by Russia to the northeast, Ukraine to the south, Poland to the west, and Lithuania and Latvia to the northwest

Source:globalsecurity.org.

of its territory to Poland after the Polish-Soviet war of 1919 to 1921, with most of the borders of Belarus adopting their modern shape in 1939 when some lands of the Second Polish Republic were reintegrated into it after the Soviet invasion of Poland and were finalized after World War II.[17,18]

During World War II, military operations devastated Belarus, which lost about a third of its population and more than half of its economic resources.[19] The republic was redeveloped in the postwar years. In 1945 Belarus became a founding member of the UN, along with the Soviet Union and the Ukrainian SSR. Later, during the dissolution of the Soviet Union the parliament of the republic declared the sovereignty of Belarus, in July 1990, becoming independence on August 25, 1991.

As per data from the U.S. government,[20] most of the Belarusian economy remains state controlled and has been described as "Soviet-style." In

[17] A Taylor & Francis Group 2004. *Europa World Year, Book 1*. Abingdon, UK: Europa publications.

[18] Abdelal, R. 2001. *National Purpose in the World Economy: Post-Soviet States in Comparative Perspective*. Ithaca, NY: Cornell University Press.

[19] Axell, A. 2002. *Russia's Heroes, 1941–45*, 247. New York, NY: Carroll & Graf Publishers.

[20] U.S. State Department 2014. "U.S. Relations with Belarus," http://state.gov/r/pa/ei/bgn/5371.htm, last accessed on 02/01/2016.

2006, foreign companies employed state-controlled companies employed 51.2 percent of Belarusians, 47.4 percent were employed by private companies, of which 5.7 percent were partially foreign owned. Important agricultural products include potatoes and cattle byproducts, including meat.[21]

After the fall of the Soviet Union, all former Soviet republics faced a deep economic crisis. Belarus has however chosen its own way of overcoming this crisis. After the 1994 election of Alexander Lukashenko as the country's first president, he launched the country on a path of "market socialism" as opposed to what Lukashenko considered "wild capitalism" chosen by Russia at that time. In keeping with this policy, administrative controls over prices and currency exchange rates were then introduced. Also, the state's right to intervene in the management of private enterprise was expanded, but on March 4, 2008, the president issues a decree abolishing the golden share rule in a clear movement to improve its international rating regarding the foreign investment.

Historically, textiles and wood processing had constituted a large part of the industrial activity in the country. Belarus's main exports included heavy machinery, agricultural products, and energy products. At the time of the dissolution of the Soviet Union in 1991, Belarus was one of the world's most industrially developed states by percentage of GDP as well as the richest CIS member state. Economically, Belarus involved itself in the CIS, Eurasian Economic Community, and Union with Russia.

The currency, the Belarusian ruble (BYR), was introduced in May 1992, replacing the Soviet ruble. The first coins of the Republic of Belarus were issued on December 27, 1996. The ruble was reintroduced with new values in 2000 and has been in use ever since. As part of the Union of Russia and Belarus, both states have discussed using a single currency along the same lines as the Euro. This led to a proposal that the Belarusian ruble be discontinued in favor of the Russian ruble (RUB), starting as early as January 1, 2008. The National Bank of Belarus abandoned pegging the Belarusian ruble to the Russian ruble in August 2007. A new

---

[21] Al Jazeera 2009. Belarus shuns Moscow amid loan row, http://aljazeera.com/news/europe/2009/05/2009529121949669957.html, last accessed on 01/28/2015.

currency, the new Belarusian ruble (BYN) will be introduced in July 2016, replacing the Belarusian ruble in a rate of 1:10,000 (10,000 old rubles = 1 new ruble). This redenomination can be considered an effort to fight the high inflation rate.

Regarding GDP growth, back in the 1990s-industrial production had plunged due to decreases in imports, investment, and demand for Belarusian products from its trading partners, which impacted GDP growth. But as depicted in Figure A.6, GDP began rising again in 1996, when Belarus became the fastest-recovering former Soviet republic in the terms of its economy. The GDP per capita in Belarus was last recorded at $17,348.77 in 2014, when adjusted by PPP, which is equivalent to 98 percent of the world's average.[22]

In 2006, Belarus's largest trading partner was Russia, which accounted for nearly half of total trade, with the EU was the next largest trading partner, with nearly a third of foreign trade. In 2005, about a quarter of the population was employed by industrial factories but employment was, and continue to be, high in agriculture, manufacturing sales, trading goods, and education. Because of its failure to protect labor rights for a labor force of more than 4 million people, among whom women hold slightly more jobs than men, Belarus lost its EU Generalized System of

BELARUS GDP PER CAPTIA PPP

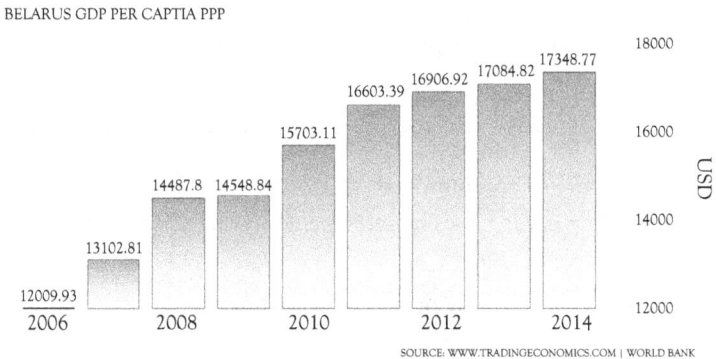

SOURCE: WWW.TRADINGECONOMICS.COM | WORLD BANK

Figure A.6 Belarus GDP per capital in PPP terms 1990–2015

Source: World Bank, tradingeconomics.

[22] Blejer, M.I., and K. Marko. 2002. *Transition: The First Decade.* Cambridge, MA: The MIT Press.

Preferences status in June 2007, which raised tariff rates to their prior most favored nation levels.[23]

Weak external demand from the key trading partners of Russia and Ukraine has depressed Belarus' output in early 2015. In addition, despite tightening of monetary policy, inflation has been high due to the impact from exchange rate depreciation. Although net exports slightly improved, foreign exchange reserves declined due to large external debt repayments. Despite the weaker economy, the government has managed to keep fiscal policy prudent. Stability-oriented macroeconomic tightening has occurred in response to a deteriorating external environment. The economy was expected to enter a recession during 2015, which was likely to endure in 2016. The current economic challenges and domestic structural constraints reinforce the need for a comprehensive economic transformation.

Georgia

Georgia is a country in Eurasia, located on the crossroads of the CIS and West Asia. As depicted in Figure A.7, the country is nestled between the Greater Caucasus and Lesser Caucasus mountain ranges. It is bordered to the west by the Black Sea, to the north and northeast by Russia, to the south by Turkey and Armenia, and to the southeast by Azerbaijan. The capital and largest city is Tbilisi. Georgia covers a territory of 69,700 square kilometers (26,911 sq. mi.), and its 2015 population is about 3.75 million. Georgia is a unitary, semipresidential republic, with the government elected through a representative democracy.

During classical antiquity, several independent kingdoms became established in what is now Georgia, including the kingdoms of Colchis and Iberia, which adopted Christianity as their state religion in the early 4th century, leading to the decline and elimination of previously dominant paganism, Zoroastrianism, and Mithraism. Thereafter and throughout the early modern period Georgia became fractured and fell into decline due to the onslaught of various hostile empires, including the Mongols, the Ottoman Empire, and successive dynasties of Iran. After a

---

[23] WTO 2012. Accessions: Belarus. https://wto.org/English/thewto_e/acc_e/a1_belarus_e.htm, last accessed on 01/28/2016.

Figure A.7 Georgia is bordered by the Black Sea on the west, to the north and northeast by Russia, to the south by Turkey and Armenia, and to the southeast by Azerbaijan

Source: RandMcnally.

brief period of independence following the Russian Revolution of 1917, the first Georgian Republic was occupied by Soviet Russia in 1921, and absorbed into the Soviet Union as the Georgian Soviet Socialist Republic in 1922. After restoring its independence in 1991, post-communist Georgia suffered from a civil unrest and economic crisis for most of the 1990s. After a peaceful change of power in the Rose Revolution of 2003, Georgia pursued a strongly pro-Western foreign policy, introducing a series of political and economic reforms.

Georgia is a member of the Council of Europe and the GUAM Organization for Democracy and Economic Development. It contains two de facto independent regions, Abkhazia and South Ossetia, which gained limited international recognition after the 2008 Russo-Georgian War. Georgia and a major part of the international community consider the regions to be part of Georgia's sovereign territory under Russian military occupation.

In February 1921, the Red Army attacked Georgia defeating the Georgian army and prompting the Social-Democratic government to flee the country. By the end of February 1921, the Red Army entered Tbilisi and installed a communist government loyal to Moscow, led by a Georgian Bolshevik named Filipp Makharadze. There remained, however, significant opposition to the Bolsheviks, which culminated in the August 1924 Uprising. Soviet rule was firmly established only after this uprising was suppressed.[24] Georgia was then incorporated into the Transcaucasian Socialist Federative Soviet Republic (TSFSR), which united Georgia, Armenia, and Azerbaijan. Later, in 1936, the TSFSR was disaggregated into its component elements and Georgia became the Georgian SSR.

Joseph Stalin, an ethnic Georgian born Ioseb Besarionis Dze Jugashvili in Gori, was prominent among the Bolsheviks. Stalin was to rise to the highest position, leading the Soviet Union from April 3, 1922 until his death on March 5, 1953. Few years later, for most of the World War II period, during 1941 to 1945, almost 700,000 Georgians fought in the Red Army against Nazi Germany, even though a few fought on the German side. About 350,000 Georgians died in the battlefields of the Eastern Front.

Georgia's main economic activities include cultivation of agricultural products such as grapes, citrus fruits, and hazelnuts, as well as mining of manganese, copper, and gold. It also produces alcoholic and nonalcoholic beverages, metals, machinery, and chemicals in small-scale industries. The country imports nearly all its needed supplies of natural gas and oil products. It has sizeable hydropower capacity that now provides most of its energy needs. Georgia has overcome the chronic energy shortages and gas supply interruptions of the past by renovating hydropower plants and by increasingly relying on natural gas imports from Azerbaijan instead of from Russia.

Despite the severe damage the economy of Georgia suffered due to civil strife in the 1990s, the country has recovered significantly by 2000, with the help of the IMF and World Bank. As depicted in Figure A.8, robust GDP growth has been achieved since then. GDP growth, spurred by gains in the industrial and service sectors, remaining in the 9 to

---

[24] Knight, A. 1995. *Beria: Stalin's First Lieutenant*, 237. Princeton, New Jersey: Princeton University Press.

GEORGIA GDP PER CAPTIA PPP

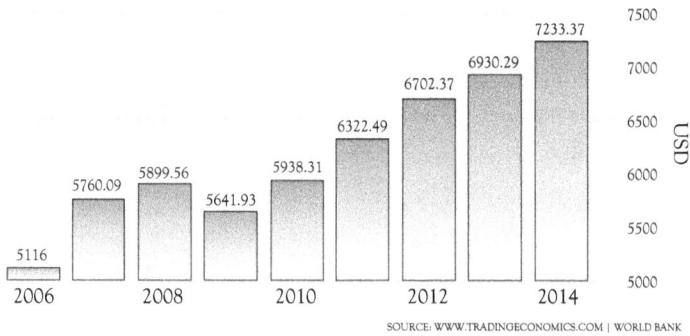

SOURCE: WWW.TRADINGECONOMICS.COM | WORLD BANK

Figure A.8 Georgia GDP growth in PPP, period 2006–2014

Source: World Bank, tradingeconomics.

12 percent range in 2005 to 07, but during 2006 and in 2008, the World Bank named Georgia the top reformer in the world.[25]

Favorable domestic conditions and strong external demand supported economic growth in the first half of this year, demonstrating that regional economic tensions have not yet adversely affected Georgia. The large Russian market, which opened for Georgian products in July 2015, helped increase exports, particularly of wine. Greater consumer and business confidence gave a boost to manufacturing and trade. In addition, the construction sector benefited from renewed public infrastructure projects and resumption in business related investments. The agricultural sector grew at a relatively modest pace compared with industry and services.

GDP growth did slow in the first quarter of 2015 to 3.2 percent from 4.8 percent for the whole of 2014. Preliminary data show a further slowdown to 2.6 percent in the first half of 2015. The slowdown largely reflects declines of 5.2 percent in manufacturing and 2.5 percent in trade, and it came despite strong growth of 22.9 percent in mining and 17.2 percent in construction. After expanding by 12.2 percent in the first quarter, bank credit fell by 1.5 percent in the second in line with slower growth.

Annual average inflation in August 2015 amounted to 3.2 percent as large increases for tobacco and alcoholic beverages and furnishings,

---

[25] World Bank 2015. "Doing Business: Georgia is This Year's Top Reformer." http://worldbank.org/en/country/georgia/overview, last accessed on 01/28/2016.

household equipment, and maintenance offset smaller declines for transport and clothing and footwear. Continuing moderate inflation, despite depreciation of the Georgia lari by nearly 33 percent since November 2014, reflects weakening domestic demand and reduced profit margins for firms, along with lower prices for imported food and energy. Inflationary expectations have recently increased, however, with the depletion of inventories accumulated at cheaper prices, rising production costs, and extensive dollarization in the economy.

Though export data for the first 6 months of 2015 suggested a further cut in exports of nearly 24 percent, reflecting a drop-in vehicle exports by nearly two-thirds, lower oil prices helped cut imports by about 9 percent. In addition, sharp declines in remittances, from the Russian Federation and Greece by 41 and 19 percent, respectively, caused total remittances to fall by almost 23 percent in the first half of 2015.

Despite planned fiscal consolidation, capital spending is expected to contribute to growth in the second half of 2015 and in 2016. However, net exports will remain a drag on growth, as recession in the Russian Federation and Ukraine weakens the external outlook. Inflation is expected to accelerate to about 6 percent by the end of 2016. With tighter monetary policy, according to the Asian Development Bank[26] outlook for Georgia in 2015 and 2016, the current account deficit may reach 14.1 percent of GDP in the first quarter of 2016 as the trade deficit widened and the regional economic slowdown trimmed remittances. The deficit was funded largely through foreign direct investment inflows and official development assistance.

Georgia has a developed, stable, and reliable energy sector but efforts are required to improve the efficiency in domestic energy use. The most promising source of additional energy generation is hydropower and the Government is focused on securing private investments for construction of new hydropower stations. Currently, only 12 percent of Georgia's hydropower potential is being utilized.

One of the potential drivers of economic growth in cities and regions is tourism, which recently saw rapid growth in Georgia and has become

---

[26] http://adA.org/countries/georgia/economy

an important source of job creation. The number of visitors increased from 560,000 in 2005 to 5 million in 2015, with 6.3 million expected in 2015. An integrated and demand-driven approach to regional development has been designed with the support of the Bank and is currently seen as critical in spurring growth and job creation in historic cities and cultural villages.

Kazakhstan

Kazakhstan, the world's largest landlocked country by land area, is a country in Central Asia, with a minor part west of the Ural River and thus in Europe. As depicted in Figure A.9, the country borders Russia on the north, China on the east, Kyrgyzstan, Uzbekistan, and Turkmenistan on the south, and the Caspian Sea on the west.

The terrain of Kazakhstan includes flatlands, steppe, taiga, rock canyons, hills, deltas, snow-capped mountains, and deserts. With an estimated 18 million people, as of 2014, Kazakhstan is the 61st most populous country in the world. Given its large land area, its population density is among the lowest, at less than 6 people per square kilometer (15 people per sq. mi.). The capital is Astana, where it was moved in 1997

Figure A.9 Kazakhstan borders Russia on the north, China on the east, Kyrgyzstan, Uzbekistan, and Turkmenistan on the south, and the Caspian Sea on the west

Source: Eurasianet.org.

from Almaty. Nomadic tribes have historically inhabited the territory of Kazakhstan. This changed in the 13th century, when Genghis Khan occupied the country as part of the Mongolian Empire.

Following internal struggles among the conquerors, power eventually reverted to the nomads. By the 16th century, the Kazakh emerged as a distinct group, divided into three jüz (ancestor branches occupying specific territories). The Russians began advancing into the Kazakh steppe in the 18th century, and by the mid-19th century, they nominally ruled all of Kazakhstan as part of the Russian Empire. Following the 1917 Russian Revolution and subsequent civil war, the territory of Kazakhstan was reorganized several times. In 1936 it was made the Kazakh Soviet Socialist Republic, considered an integral part of the Soviet Union.

Kazakhstan was the last of the Soviet republics to declare independence following the dissolution of the Soviet Union in 1991. Kazakhstan has worked to develop its economy, especially its dominant hydrocarbon industry.[27] Human Rights Watch says that "Kazakhstan heavily restricts freedom of assembly, speech, and religion,[28]" and other human rights organizations regularly describe Kazakhstan's human rights situation as poor.

The country is populated by 131 ethnicities, including Kazakhs (who make up 63 percent of the population), Russians, Uzbeks, Ukrainians, Germans, Tatars, and Uyghurs. Islam is the religion of about 70 percent of the population, with Christianity practiced by 26 percent. Kazakhstan officially allows freedom of religion, but religious leaders who oppose the government are suppressed. The Kazakh language is the state language, and Russian has equal official status for all levels of administrative and institutional purposes, reflecting the long history of Russian dominance in the region.

Kazakhstan is an upper-middle-income country with per capita GDP adjusted for PPP, as depicted in Figure A.10, of nearly $22,469 thousand

[27] Zarakhovich, Y. 2006. "Kazakhstan Comes on Strong." *Time*, http://content.time.com/time/world/article/0,8599,1539999,00.html, last accessed on 01/28/2016.

[28] Human Rights Watch, World Report 2015. Kazakhstan, https://hrw.org/world-report/2015/country-chapters/kazakhstan, last accessed 01/28/2016.

KAZAKHSTAN GDP PER CAPTIA PPP

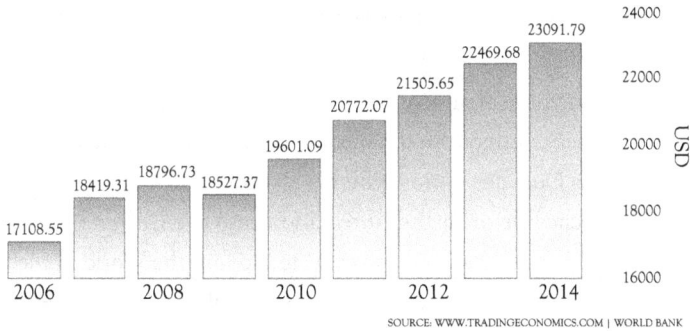

Figure A.10 Kazakhstan GDP per capita PPP 2006–2014

Source: World Bank, tradingeconomics.

in 2015. Its per capita GDP grew in 2014 although real GDP dropped due to internal capacity constraints in the oil industry, less favorable terms of trade, and an economic slowdown in Russia. The contribution of net exports to GDP growth improved materially followed by a sharp devaluation of the Kazakhstan tenge in February 2014, leading to a strong drop in imports of goods that became costlier. Because of the devaluation, domestic inflation, as measured by the consumer price index (CPI), increased from 4.8 percent year-on-year in December 2015 to 6.9 percent in August 2014, due to higher imported input prices.

Income growth in the country had a positive impact on poverty indicators, with prosperity shared broadly. The share of the Kazakhstan population living in poverty went down from 47 percent in 2001 to about 3 percent in 2015, as measured by the national poverty line. Similarly, at the international poverty line, as measured by the PPP-corrected $2.50 per capita per day, poverty in Kazakhstan fell from 41 percent in 2001 to 4 percent in 2009.

However, against a benchmark of a higher poverty line at the PPP-corrected $5 per capita per day (which is more appropriate for countries with a higher level of income per capita), some 42 percent of Kazakhstan's population were still living in poverty in 2009, though down from 79 percent in 2001. Kazakhstan's performance in the World Bank's indicator of shared prosperity also shows progress, with growth rate of consumption per capita of the bottom 40 percent of households of about

6 percent, while the average consumption growth for all households was about 5 percent during 2006 to 2010.

Trade policy will remain a central instrument to help the country integrate into the global economy, but Kazakhstan will face a complex trade policy environment in the medium term. The economy is adjusting to the Eurasia Customs Union which it joined in 2010 and is pursuing an accelerated schedule of further integration into the Common Economic Space by 2015. Kazakhstan is also expected to join the World Trade Organization soon while its trade strategy lists several free trade agreements to be negotiated.

Education is a high priority for Kazakhstan, and in 2011, Kazakhstan ranked first on UNESCO's "Education for All Development Index" by achieving near-universal levels of primary education, adult literacy, and gender parity. These results have reflected Kazakhstan's efforts of expanding preschool access and free, compulsory secondary education. For the next 10 years, Kazakhstan is embarking on further major reforms across all education levels.

Kazakhstan faces challenges in restructuring its health care system. The country's health outcomes lag its rapidly increasing income. The major causes of adult mortality are noncommunicable diseases such as cancer, cardiovascular disease, and other tobacco and alcohol-related diseases and injuries. The new State Health Care Development Program recognizes health as one of the country's major priorities and a prerequisite for sustainable socioeconomic development.

Looking forward, despite the short-term vulnerabilities accentuated by the uncertain regional economic outlook, Kazakhstan's medium-term prospects look promising. In the medium term, the economy will continue to grow on the back of the expanding oil sector, while growth of the nonoil economy will be lower due to lower domestic demand. In the longer run, Kazakhstan's development objective of joining the rank of the top 30 most developed countries by 2050 will depend on its ability to sustain balanced and inclusive growth. Enhancing medium- to long-term development prospects depends on Kazakhstan's success in diversifying its endowments, namely, creating highly skilled human capital, improving the quality of physical capital, and more importantly, strengthening institutional capital—all the necessary ingredients for the development and expansion of the private sector in the country.

Kyrgyzstan

Kyrgyzstan's history spans over 2,000 years, encompassing a variety of cultures and empires. Although geographically isolated by its highly mountainous terrain, which has helped preserve its ancient culture, Kyrgyzstan has historically been at the crossroads of several great civilizations, namely as part of the Silk Road and other commercial and cultural routes. Though long inhabited by a succession of independent tribes and clans, Kyrgyzstan has periodically come under foreign domination and attained sovereignty as a nation state only after the breakup of the Soviet Union in 1991.

The country, officially known as Kyrgyz Republic, is a country located in Central Asia. As depicted in Figure A.11, the country is landlocked and mountainous, bordered by Kazakhstan to the north, Uzbekistan to the west, and Tajikistan to the southwest and China to the east. Its capital and largest city is Bishkek.

Since independence, Kyrgyzstan has officially been a unitary parliamentary republic, although it continues to endure ethnic conflicts, revolts, economic troubles, transitional governments, and political party

Figure A.11 Kyrgyzstan is bordered by Kazakhstan to the north, Uzbekistan to the west, Tajikistan to the southwest and China to the east

conflicts.[29] Kyrgyzstan is a member of the CIS, the Eurasian Economic Union, the Collective Security Treaty Organization, the Shanghai Cooperation Organization, the Organization of Islamic Cooperation, the Turkic Council, the TÜRKSOY community, and the UN.

Ethnic Kyrgyz make up much of the country's 5.7 million people, followed by significant minorities of Uzbeks and Russians. The official language, Kyrgyz, is closely related to the other Turkic languages, although Russian remains widely spoken, a legacy of a century-long policy of *Russification*. Most of the population, about 64 percent, is nondenominational Muslims. In addition to its Turkic origins, Kyrgyz culture bears elements of Persian, Mongolian, and Russian influence.

After independence in 1992, the Kyrgyz Republic's economy and public services were hit hard by the breakup of the Soviet economic zone and the end of subsidies from Moscow. Thanks to the adoption of market-based economic reforms in the 1990s, the economy has nearly recovered to its pre-independence level of output, but infrastructure and social services have suffered from low investment. With a per capita PPP GDP of $2,920.60 in 2011, as depicted in Figure A.12, the Kyrgyz Republic remains a low-income country. Moreover, the global economic crisis, the political unrest of April and June 2010 and food price increases

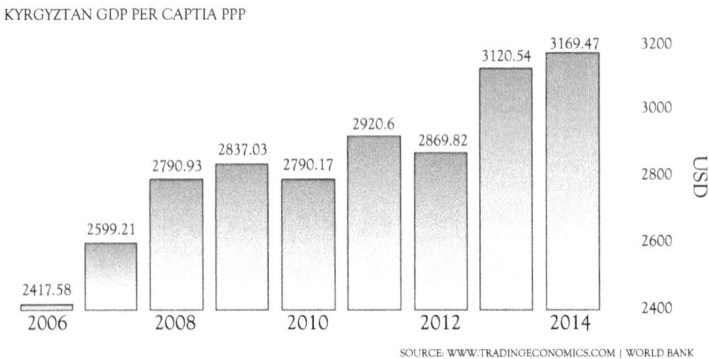

KYRGYZTAN GDP PER CAPTIA PPP

SOURCE: WWW.TRADINGECONOMICS.COM | WORLD BANK

Figure A.12 Kyrgyzstan per capita GDP 2006–2014

Source: World Bank, tradingeconomics.

[29] The Economist 2011. "Investigating Kyrgyzstan's ethnic violence: Bloody business." *The Economist*, http://economist.com/node/18682522, last accessed on 01/28/2016.

in 2011 and 2012 have reversed earlier gains in poverty reduction with GDP dropping to $2,869.82. The absolute poverty rate increased from 33.7 percent in 2010 to 36.8 percent in 2011.

A series of reform-oriented government policies since the political crises of 2010, have sought to restore economic and social stability, and to address shortcomings in public governance and the investment climate. Following strong growth in 2015, the Kyrgyz economy was hit by a significant decline in gold production due to geological movements at the Kumtor gold mine. Real GDP in the first half of 2012 contracted by 5.6 percent as gold production at Kumtor fell by 60 percent. Excluding Kumtor, real output grew moderately at 3.9 percent with growth across all sectors.

Weak economic governance and a high level of perceived corruption remain key obstacles to development in the Kyrgyz Republic, and were considered causes of the political unrest of 2010. The government's Medium Term Development Program, adopted in 2011, stated improving governance and fighting corruption to be its top priority.

The agricultural sector, which accounts for about a quarter of the country's GDP and about one third of employment, expanded rapidly between 1996 and 2002. The Government successfully completed a land reform, created a rural bank and agribusiness or rural advisory services, and established water-user associations and pasture committees. The energy sector is one of the largest in the Kyrgyz economy, accounting for around 3.9 percent of GDP and 16 percent of industrial production. The bulk of the country's current generating capacity is hydropower. The key challenges faced by the sector are high commercial losses and low tariffs, leading to inadequate funding for maintenance and investment, winter energy shortages, and governance issues. All these led to significant deterioration of energy assets and poor sector performance. Mining constitutes about 26 percent of tax revenues, about 10 percent of GDP, and 50 percent of export earnings. The country has been reviewing mining legislation and mineral licensing procedures. To address governance issues in mining, the Kyrgyz Government started implementing the Extractive Industries Transparency Initiative in 2004.

The road network connects remote communities and links the Kyrgyz Republic to neighboring countries. Rehabilitating strategic road corridors is on the Government's priority list, given their importance in providing access to international markets and basic public services. However, basic preventative maintenance is seriously underfunded.

Improving education, health care and social protection is another top priority for the Kyrgyz Republic. The Government is currently implementing medium term reforms in these sectors.

Moldova

Moldova, as depicted in Figure A.13, is a landlocked country in the CIS, bordered by Romania to the west and Ukraine to the north, east, and south. The capital city is Chişinău. Moldova is a parliamentary republic

Figure A.13 Moldova is a landlocked country in The CIS, bordered by Romania to the west and Ukraine to the north, east, and south

Source: Magellan Geographix.

with a president as head of state and a prime minister as head of government. It is a member state of the UN, the Council of Europe, the WTO, the OSCE, the GUUAM (Georgia, Ukraine, Uzbekistan, Azerbaijan, and Moldova), the CIS and the Organization of the Black Sea Economic Cooperation (BSEC) and aspires to join the EU.

Moldova declared independence on August 27, 1991 as part of the dissolution of the Soviet Union. The current Constitution of Moldova was adopted in 1994. A strip of Moldovan territory on the east bank of the river Dniester has been under the de facto control of the breakaway government of Transnistria since 1990, which includes a large proportion of predominantly russophone East Slavs of Ukrainian (28 percent) and Russian (26 percent) descent (altogether 54 percent as of 1989), while Moldovans (40 percent) have been the largest ethnic group, and where the headquarters and many units of the Soviet 14th Guards Army were stationed, an independent Pridnestrovian Moldavian Soviet Socialist Republic was proclaimed on August 16, 1990, with its capital in Tiraspol.

The motives behind this move were fear of the rise of nationalism in Moldova and the country's expected reunification with Romania upon secession from the USSR. In the winter of 1991 to 1992 clashes occurred between Transnistrian forces, supported by elements of the 14th Army, and the Moldovan police. Between March 2 and July 26, 1992, the conflict escalated into a military engagement.

After the breakup from the USSR in 1991, energy shortages, political uncertainty, trade obstacles and weak administrative capacity contributed to the decline of economy. In January 1992, Moldova introduced a market economy, liberalizing prices, which resulted in rapid inflation. As a part of an ambitious economic liberalization effort, Moldova introduced a convertible currency, liberalized all prices, stopped issuing preferential credits to state enterprises, backed steady land privatization, removed export controls, and liberalized interest rates. The government entered agreements with the World Bank and the International Monetary Fund to promote growth. The economy reversed from decline in late 1990s.

From 1992 to 2001, the country suffered a serious economic crisis, leaving most of the population below the poverty line. In 1993, a national

currency, the Moldovan leu, was introduced to replace the temporary cou-
pon. The economy of Moldova began to change in 2001, and until 2008
the country saw a steady annual growth of between 5 and 10 percent.

The early 2000s also saw a considerable growth of emigration of Moldovans looking for work in Russia, Italy, Portugal, Spain, Greece, Cyprus,
Turkey, and other countries. Thus, remittances from Moldovans abroad
account for almost 38 percent of Moldova's GDP, the second-highest
percentage in the world, after Tajikistan. Due to a decrease in industrial
and agricultural output following the dissolution of the Soviet Union,
the service sector has grown to dominate Moldova's economy and currently composes over 60 percent of the nation's GDP. However, Moldova
remains the poorest country in Europe.

Moldova's economic performance over the last few years, as depicted
in Figure A.14, has been relatively strong, aided by improved fiscal, monetary and exchange rate policy. Moldova experienced the highest cumulative per capita PPP GDP growth, relative to the precrisis year of 2007,
in the region. However, growth has been volatile because of climatic and
global economic conditions. The GDP per capita in Moldova was last
recorded at $4,753.55 in 2014, when adjusted by PPP. The GDP per cap-
ita, in the country, when adjusted by PPP is equivalent to 27 percent of
the world's average. GDP per capita PPP in Moldova averaged $3,476.80
from 1990 until 2014, reaching an all-time high of $6,416.46 in 1990
and a record low of $2,267.88 in 1999.

MOLDOVA GDP PER CAPTIA PPP

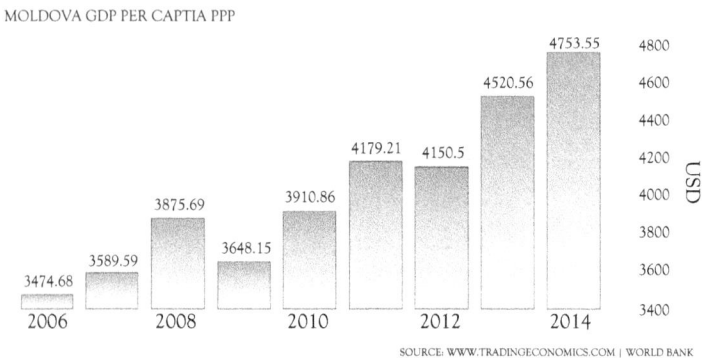

Figure A.14 Moldova's per capita PPP GDP 2006–2015

Source: World Bank, tradingeconomics.com.

However, the economy decreased 3.7 percent in the third quarter of 2015. Due to a bad harvest, agriculture decreased 17.4 percent and on the expenditure, side the internal demand was weak due to low remittances. Nonetheless, good economic performance in the first half of the year, maintained Moldova's GDP growth positive, increasing 0.5 percent, y/y, in January to September 2015.

The existing macroeconomic framework is considered broadly adequate, even though macroeconomic risks associated with the financial sector, vulnerabilities to external and climatic shocks, institutional weaknesses and related slippages in the implementation of macroeconomic and structural reforms will continue to be substantial over the medium term. European integration anchors the Government's policy reform agenda, but political tensions and weak governance pose risks to reforms.

Moldova's recent economic performance reduced poverty and promoted shared prosperity. The national poverty and extreme poverty rates, using national poverty definitions, fell from 30.2 and 4.5 percent in 2006 to 16.6 and 0.6 percent respectively in 2012, making Moldova one of the world's top performers in terms of poverty reduction. Similarly, consumption growth among the bottom 40 percent of the population outpaced average consumption growth.

Despite a sharp decline in poverty, however, Moldova remains one of the poorest countries in Europe. The most vulnerable groups at risk of poverty in Moldova remain those with low education levels, households with three or more children, those in rural areas, families relying on self-employment, the elderly, and Roma. Additionally, the reduction in remittances could negatively impact consumption and poverty. Moldova performs well in some areas of gender equality, yet disparities persist in education, health, economic opportunity, agency, and violence against women. Human trafficking is a serious problem; Moldova is a source, and to a lesser extent a transit and destination country, for both sex trafficking and forced labor.

Considering the fragile economic and political external environment the pace of reforms must be accelerated. Key challenges include fighting corruption, improving the investment climate, removing obstacles for exporters, channeling remittances into productive investments, and developing a sound financial sector. Moldova needs to improve the efficiency and equity of its public spending, through better management of public capital investments, which are crucial for higher growth. Administrative and judicial reforms remain a challenge for improving public sector governance, which is a precondition for European integration and economic modernization.

Russia

Russia, a federal semipresidential republic, is a country in northern Eurasia, the largest country in the world, covering more than one-eighth of the Earth's inhabited land area. Russia is the world's ninth most populous country with over 144 million people at the end of 2015. Extending across the entirety of northern Asia and much of The CIS, Russia spans over 11 time zones and incorporates a wide range of environments and landforms. As depicted in Figure A.15, from northwest to southeast, Russia is boarded by Norway, Finland, Estonia, Latvia, Lithuania,

Figure A.15 Russia is boarded by Norway, Finland, Estonia, Latvia, Lithuania, Poland, Belarus, and Ukraine to the west; Georgia, Azerbaijan, Kazakhstan, China, Mongolia, and North Korea to the south; and the North Pacific Ocean to the east; it shares maritime borders with Japan by the Sea of Okhotsk and the U.S. state of Alaska across the Bering Strait

Source: Russialist.org.

Poland, Belarus, and Ukraine on the west, Georgia, Azerbaijan, Kazakhstan, China, Mongolia, and North Korea to the south, and the North Pacific Ocean to the east. It shares maritime borders with Japan by the Sea of Okhotsk and the U.S. state of Alaska across the Bering Strait.

The nation's history began with that of the East Slavs, who emerged as a recognizable group in Europe between the 3rd and 8th centuries AD. Founded and ruled by a Varangian warrior elite and their descendants, the medieval state of Rus arose in the 9th century. In 988 it adopted Orthodox Christianity from the Byzantine Empire, beginning the synthesis of Byzantine and Slavic cultures that defined Russian culture for the next millennium. Rus' ultimately disintegrated into several smaller states; most of the Rus' lands were overrun by the Mongol invasion and became tributaries of the nomadic Golden Horde in the 13th century.

The Grand Duchy of Moscow gradually reunified the surrounding Russian principalities, achieved independence from the Golden Horde, and came to dominate the cultural and political legacy of Kievan Rus.' By the 18th century, the nation had greatly expanded through conquest, annexation, and exploration to become the Russian Empire, which was the third largest empire in history, stretching from Poland in Europe to Alaska in North America.[30]

Following the Russian Revolution, the Russian Soviet Federative Socialist Republic became the largest and leading constituent of the Soviet Union, the world's first constitutionally socialist state and a recognized world superpower, and a rival to the United States,[31] which played a decisive role in the Allied victory in World War II. The Soviet era saw some of the most significant technological achievements of the 20th century, including the world's first human-made satellite, and the first man in space. By the end of 1990, the Soviet Union had the world's second largest economy, largest standing military in the world and the largest stockpile of weapons of mass destruction.

---

[30] Taagepera, R. 1997. "Expansion and Contraction Patterns of Large Polities: Context for Russia." *International Studies Quarterly* 41, no. 3, pp. 475–504.
[31] Adelman, J.R., and C.L. Gibson. 1989. *Contemporary Soviet Military Affairs: The Legacy of World War II*, 4. Unwin Hyman.

Following the partition of the Soviet Union in 1991, 14 Independent republic nations emerged from the USSR, including Armenia, Azerbaijan, Belarus, Estonia, Georgia, Kazakhstan, Kyrgyzstan, Latvia, Lithuania, Moldova, Tajikistan, Turkmenistan, Ukraine, Uzbekistan. As the largest, most populous, and most economically developed republic, the Russian Soviet Federative Socialist Republic (SFSR) reconstituted itself as the Russian Federation and is recognized as the continuing legal personality of the Soviet Union.

The Russian economy ranks as the tenth largest by nominal GDP and sixth largest by PPP as of 2015.[32] Russia's extensive mineral and energy resources, the largest reserves in the world, have made it one of the largest producers of oil and natural gas globally.[33] The country is one of the five recognized nuclear weapons states and possesses the largest stockpile of weapons of mass destruction. Russia was the world's second biggest exporter of major arms in 2010 to 2014, per Stockholm International Peace Research Institute (SIPRI) data.[34]

Russia is a great power and a permanent member of the UN Security Council, a member of the G20, the Council of Europe, the Asia-Pacific Economic Cooperation (APEC), the Shanghai Cooperation Organization (SCO), the Organization for Security and Cooperation in Europe (OSCE), and the World Trade Organization (WTO), as well as being the leading member of the CIS, the Collective Security Treaty Organization (CSTO) and one of the five members of the Eurasian Economic Union (EEU), along with Armenia, Belarus, Kazakhstan, and Kyrgyzstan.

Russia has a developed, high-income market economy with enormous natural resources, particularly oil and natural gas. It has the 15th largest economy in the world by nominal GDP and the 6th largest by PPP. As

---

[32] IMF 2015."Report for Selected Countries and Subjects." http://imf.org/external/pubs/ft/weo/2015/01/weodata/index.aspx, last accessed on 01/28/2016.

[33] International Energy Agency 2012. "Oil Market Report." https://weA.archive.org/web/20120518015934/http://omrpublic.iea.org/omrarchive/18jan12sup.pdf, last accessed 01/28/2016.

[34] Stockholm International Peace Research Institute 2014. "Trends in International Arms Transfer, 2014." http://books.sipri.org/product_info?c_product_id=495, last accessed 01/28/16.

RUSSIA GDP PER CAPTIA PPP

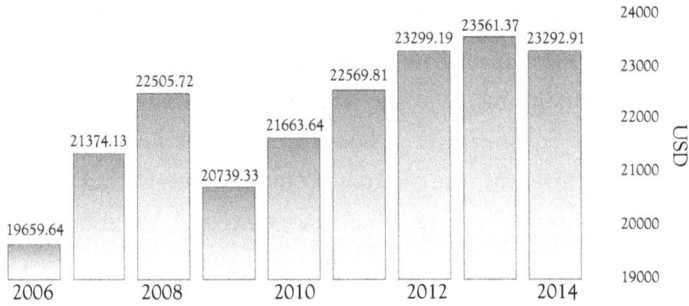

Figure A.16 Russia's per capita PPP GDP 2006–2015

Source: World Bank, tradingeconomics.com

depicted in Figure A.16, since the turn of the 21st century, higher domestic consumption and greater political stability have bolstered economic growth in Russia. The GDP per capita in Russia was last recorded at $23,292.91 in 2014, when adjusted by PPP. The GDP per capita, in Russia, when adjusted by PPP is equivalent to 131 percent of the world's average. GDP per capita PPP in Russia averaged $17,196.23 from 1990 until 2014, reaching an all-time high of $23,561.37 in 2015 and a record low of $11,173.03 in 1998.

The country ended 2008 with its 9th straight year of growth, but growth has slowed with the decline in the price of oil and gas. Non-traded services and goods for the domestic market, as opposed to oil or mineral extraction and exports, primarily drove growth. Approximately 12.8 percent of Russians lived below the national poverty line in 2011, significantly down from 40 percent in 1998 at the worst point of the post-Soviet collapse. Unemployment in Russia was 5.4 percent in 2014, down from about 12.4 percent in 1999. The middle class has grown from just 8 million persons in 2000 to 104 million persons in 2015. However, after U.S.-led sanctions since 2014 and a collapse in oil prices, the proportion of middle class could halve to 20 percent. Sugar imports reportedly dropped 82 percent between 2012 and 2015 because of the increase in domestic output.

Russia's recession deepened in the first half of 2015 with a severe impact on households. The economy continues to adjust to the 2014 terms-of-trade shock amid a tense geopolitical context marked by ongoing international sanctions. Oil and gas prices remained low through the first half of 2015, further underscoring Russia's vulnerability to volatile global commodity markets. The weakening of the ruble created a price advantage for some industries, boosting a narrow range of exports and encouraging investment in a certain sector, but this was not sufficient to generate an overall increase in nonenergy exports. Investment demand continued to contract for a third consecutive year.

Economic policy uncertainty arising from an unpredictable geopolitical situation and the continuation of the sanctions regime caused private investment to decline rapidly as capital costs rose and consumer demand evaporated. The record drop in consumer demand was driven by a sharp contraction in real wages, which fell by an average of 8.5 percent in the first 6 months of 2015, illustrating the severity of the recession. However, the deterioration of real wages was also the primary mechanism through which the labor market adjusted to lower demand, and unemployment increased only slightly from 5.3 percent in 2014 to 5.6 percent in the first half of 2015. The erosion of real income significantly increased the poverty rate and exacerbated the vulnerability of households in the lower 40 percent of the income distribution.

The policy response by the authorities successfully stabilized the economy. The transition to a free-floating exchange rate allowed imports to adjust to 17 percent depreciation in the real effective exchange rate during the first half of 2015, strengthening the current-account balance. Meanwhile, measures to support the financial sector appear to have contained systemic risks, and there are early signs of stabilization. Nevertheless, the pass-through effect of the December 2014 depreciation boosted inflation to levels not seen since 2002.

Even as the recession deepened in the first half of 2015 controlling inflation became the central bank's main policy challenge. Low oil prices continue to put downward pressure on federal revenue, ushering in a period of difficult fiscal consolidation. Real public spending is expected to fall by 5 percent in 2015, notwithstanding a temporary increase in the first half of the year caused by frontloaded expenditures as part of the government's anticrisis plan to cushion some of the fiscal consolidation impact. Falling oil revenues constrained the government's ability to counter the decline in real income, and nominal increases in pensions and social benefits were below the headline inflation rate. This accelerated an already troubling rise in the poverty rate, which climbed from 13.1 percent in the first half of 2014 to 15.1 percent in the first half of 2015.

Turkmenistan

Turkmenistan, as depicted in Figure A.17, is a country in Central Asia, bordered by Kazakhstan to the northwest, Uzbekistan to the north and east, Afghanistan to the southeast, Iran to the south and southwest, and the Caspian Sea to the west.

Turkmenistan has been at the crossroads of civilizations for centuries. In medieval times, Merv was one of the great cities of the Islamic world and an important stop on the Silk Road, a caravan route used for trade with China until the mid-15th century. Annexed by the Russian Empire in 1881, Turkmenistan later figured prominently in the anti-Bolshevik movement in Central Asia. In 1924, Turkmenistan became a constituent

Figure A.17 Turkmenistan is bordered by Kazakhstan to the northwest, Uzbekistan to the north and east, Afghanistan to the southeast, Iran to the south and southwest, and the Caspian Sea to the west

Source: Encyclopedia Britannica.

republic of the Soviet Union, Turkmen Soviet Socialist Republic (Turkmen SSR). The country became independent upon the dissolution of the Soviet Union in 1991. Turkmenistan possesses the world's fourth largest reserves of natural gas resources.[35] Most of the country is covered by the Karakum (Black Sand) Desert. Since 1993, citizens have received government-provided electricity, water, and natural gas free of charge.

President for Life Saparmurat Niyazov ruled Turkmenistan until his death in 2006. Gurbanguly Berdimuhamedow was elected president in 2007. As per Human Rights Watch, "Turkmenistan remains one of the world's most repressive countries. The country is virtually closed to independent scrutiny, media and religious freedoms are subject to draconian restrictions, and human rights defenders and other activists face the constant threat of government reprisal." President Berdymukhamedow promotes a personality cult in which he, his relatives, and associates enjoy unlimited power and total control over all aspects of public life.[36]

The Turkmen economy, as depicted in Figure A.18, continued strong growth performance in 2012, expanding by 11.1 percent. High growth

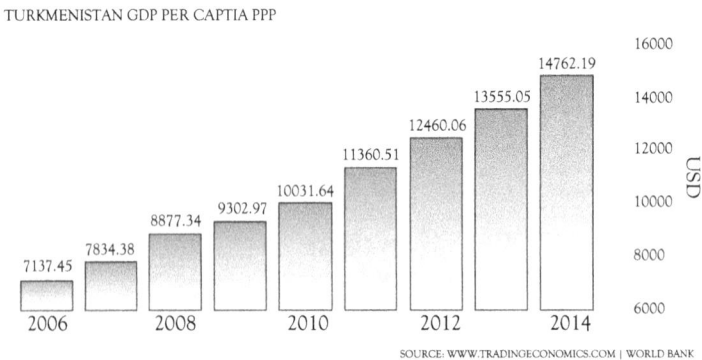

TURKMENISTAN GDP PER CAPTIA PPP

SOURCE: WWW.TRADINGECONOMICS.COM | WORLD BANK

Figure A.18 Turkmenistan GDP per capita PPP 2006–2014

Source: World Bank, tradingeconomics.com.

---

[35] Fox News 2006. "Turkmenistan's Leader Promises Citizens Free Gas, Electricity and Water Through 2030." http://foxnews.com/story/2006/10/25/turkmenistan-leader-promises-citizens-free-gas-electricity-and-water-through.html, last accessed 01/28/2016.

[36] HRW 2014. "World Report 2014: Turkmenistan." https://hrw.org/world-report/2014/country-chapters/turkmenistan, last accessed 01/28/2016.

performance sustained over an extended period led to a steady increase in income levels and moved the country to an upper middle-income status. Preliminary outcomes of the annual economic developments demonstrate that the Turkmen economy remains resilient to the global uncertainties stemming from the Eurozone crisis. The GDP per capita in Turkmenistan was last recorded at $14,762.19 in 2014, when adjusted by PPP. The GDP per capita, in Turkmenistan, when adjusted by PPP is equivalent to 83 percent of the world's average. GDP per capita PPP in Turkmenistan averaged $7,471.40 from 1990 until 2014, reaching an all-time high of $14,762.19 in 2014 and a record low of $4,221.14 in 1997.

The country possesses the world's fourth-largest reserves of natural gas and substantial oil resources. Turkmenistan has taken a cautious approach to economic reform, hoping to use gas and cotton sales to sustain its economy. In 2004, the unemployment rate was estimated to be 60 percent. However, between 1998 and 2002, Turkmenistan suffered from the continued lack of adequate export routes for natural gas and from obligations on extensive short-term external debt. At the same time, however, the value of total exports has risen sharply because of increases in international oil and gas prices. Economic prospects soon are discouraging because of widespread internal poverty and the burden of foreign debt.

The government maintains a large portfolio of social transfers and budget subsidies. Currently, all 17 subsidies have a universal character and are guaranteed until 2030, after which time the government may decide to move to a more targeted public social transfer policy. Social indicators have showed improvements commensurate with the country's economic performance. Per the State Statistics Committee of Turkmenistan, wages and salaries have increased by 11.2 percent during 2012 compared to 2011. After adjusting for inflation, the real rate of wage increase still make up 6 percent.

The Government's National Socio-Economic Development Program for 2011 to 2030 and the National Rural Development Program focus on inclusive economic growth while preserving economic independence, modernizing the country's infrastructure, and promoting foreign direct investment.

Tajikistan

Tajikistan is a mountainous landlocked sovereign country in Central Asia, with an estimated 8 million people in 2015, it is the 98th most populous country and with an area of 143,100 square kilometers (55,300 sq. mi.). It is the 96th largest country in the world. The territory that now constitutes the country was previously home to several ancient cultures, including the city of Sarazm of the Neolithic and the Bronze Age, and was later home to kingdoms ruled by people of different faiths and cultures, including the Oxus civilization, Andronovo culture, Buddhism, Nestorian Christianity, Zoroastrianism, and Manichaeism.

As depicted in Figure A.19, the country is bordered by Afghanistan to the south, Uzbekistan to the west, Kyrgyzstan to the north, and China to the east. Pakistan lies to the south separated by the narrow Wakhan Corridor. Traditional homelands of Tajik people included present-day Tajikistan, Afghanistan, and Uzbekistan.

Numerous empires and dynasties, including the Achaemenid Empire, Sassanian Empire, Hephthalite Empire, Samanid Empire, Mongol Empire, Timurid dynasty, and the Russian Empire, have ruled the area. Because of the breakup of the Soviet Union, Tajikistan became an independent nation in 1991. A civil war was fought almost immediately after

Figure A.19 Tajikistan is bordered by Afghanistan to the south, Uzbekistan to the west, Kyrgyzstan to the north, and China to the east

Source: Operationworld.com.

independence, lasting from 1992 to 1997. Since the end of the war, newly established political stability and foreign aid have allowed the country's economy to grow.

Tajikistan is a presidential republic consisting of four provinces. Most of Tajikistan's 8 million people belong to the Tajik ethnic group, who speak Tajik (Persian), although many people also speak Russian. Mountains cover more than 90 percent of the country. It has a transition economy that is dependent on aluminum and cotton production. Its economy is the 126th largest in the world in terms of purchasing power and 136th largest in terms of nominal GDP.

Because of the economic recession in Russia, weakening of the Russian ruble and tightening of migration regulations, economic growth in Tajikistan slowed from an average of 7.5 percent a year over the past decade to 6.4 percent in the first 6 months of 2015. The U.S. dollar value of remittances, about 80 percent of which originate from Russia, fell by 32 percent in January to June 2015, compared to the same period in 2014, largely due to the sharp depreciation of the Russian ruble. The slowdown in remittances affected domestic demand, which in turn depressed growth in services, the major contributor to economic growth in the past.

Growth is projected to significantly slowdown in the medium term, with a very gradual recovery, putting Tajikistan's poverty reduction gains of the last decade at great risk. As this trend in the economy is likely to persist in the medium term, it is even more important that Tajikistan implements sound macroeconomic policies and structural reforms that are necessary to create the foundation for more domestically generated inclusive growth, while investing in quality public services. The current situation should be an opportunity to reform the economy and to adopt new engines of growth—private investment and export—to generate more and better-paying jobs in the country.

To date, Tajikistan has done a remarkable job in reducing poverty. During the period 1999 to 2014, poverty fell from over 80 percent to about 32 percent in the country. Tajikistan's pace of poverty reduction over the past 15 years has been among the top 10 percent in the world. However, the country has done less well in reducing nonmonetary poverty. Recently available micro-data suggest that limited or no access to education (secondary and tertiary), heating, and sanitation is the main

TAJIKISTAN GDP PER CAPTIA PPP

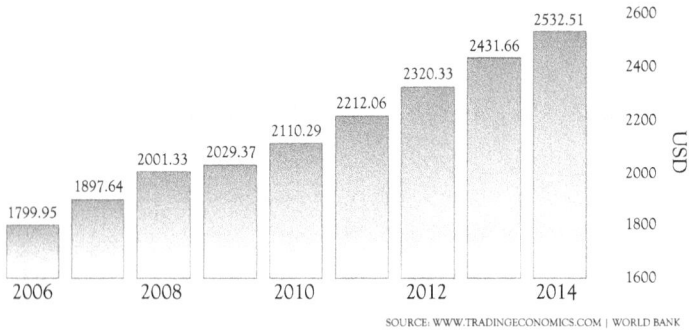

Figure A.20 Tajikistan GDP per capita PPP 2006–2015

Source: World Bank, tradingeconomics.com.

contributors to nonmonetary poverty. These three are the most unequally distributed services, with access to education varying by income level and heating and sanitation per location.

As depicted in Figure A.20, Tajikistan's GDP per capita was last recorded at $2,532.51 in 2014, when adjusted by PPP. The GDP per capita, in Tajikistan, when adjusted by PPP is equivalent to 14 percent of the world's average. GDP per capita PPP in Tajikistan averaged $1,849.28 from 1990 until 2014, reaching an all-time high of $3,635.34 in 1990 and a record low of $1,040.23 in 1996.

The Government of Tajikistan has set ambitious goals to be reached by 2020: to double GDP, to reduce poverty to 20 percent, and to expand the middle class. To achieve higher growth, Tajikistan needs to implement a deeper structural reform agenda designed to (a) reduce the role of the state and enlarge that of the private sector in the economy through a more conducive business climate, thus increasing private investment and generating more productive jobs; (b) modernize and improve the efficiency and social inclusiveness of basic public services; and (c) enhance the country's connectivity to regional and global markets and knowledge.

The difficult environment for doing business in Tajikistan, as well as obstacles to foreign direct investment, have discouraged private investment and limited overall investment. Averaging about 15 percent of GDP annually since 2008, total investment is low by regional and international standards.

Public investment accounts for 80 percent of the total, or 12 percent of GDP, and private investment for 20 percent, or only 3 percent of GDP—much lower than the Europe and Central Asia developing country average. The main obstacles cited by both local and foreign entrepreneurs are inadequate infrastructure, insufficient and unreliable energy supply, the weak rule of law, especially about property rights, and tax policy and administration. Increased private investment and new business development are crucial prerequisites for increased job creation.

With 20 percent of GDP and 53 percent of employment, the agriculture sector in Tajikistan offers a solid foundation for economic development. The Government of Tajikistan displays a strong commitment to the agricultural reform program, which includes the resolution of the cotton debt crisis, accelerated land reform, freedom to farm, improved access to rural finance, and increased diversification of agriculture.

Efforts are underway to make investment in agriculture more profitable, especially for exports, by enhancing access to markets and by empowering farmers through strengthening their land-use rights, improving their access to credit and inputs, and enabling them to make their own cropping decisions. The recent growth of non-cotton agricultural exports indicates the potential for growth in agro-processing, including storage of fruit and vegetables, which holds great promise for development, along with textiles and clothing.

Meeting Tajikistan's energy demand will be an important part of the agenda to reduce poverty and create an enabling environment for private businesses. Approximately 70 percent of the population suffers from extensive electricity shortages during winter. The shortages increased considerably starting in 2009, when Tajikistan's power network was severed from the Central Asia Power System and power trade with Central Asian countries stopped. Electricity shortages in winter are estimated to be at least 2,000 gigawatt-hours, or about 20 percent of winter electricity demand.

Tajikistan is also faced with a young and rapidly growing population. Recent estimates show that 55 percent of the population in Tajikistan is under the age of 25, making improved public services in social sectors (education, health, and social protection), as well as job creation, imperative components of Government's Poverty Reduction Strategy.

Ukraine

The territory of modern Ukraine has been inhabited since 32,000 BC. During the middle Ages, the area was a key center of East Slavic culture, with the powerful state of Kievan Rus' forming the basis of Ukrainian identity. The country is currently in dispute with Russia over the Crimean, which Russia annexed back in 2014, although Ukraine and most of the international community still do not recognize as Russian. If we include Crimea, Ukraine has a total area of 603,628 square kilometers (233,062 sq. mi.), which makes the country the largest within the entire Europe and the 46th largest country in the world. With a total population of about 44.5 million, Ukraine is the 32nd most populous country in the world. Ukraine, as depicted in Figure A.21, is a country in the CIS bordered by Russia to the east and northeast, Belarus to the northwest, Poland and Slovakia to the west, Hungary, Romania, and Moldova to the southwest, and the Black Sea and Sea of Azov to the south and southeast, respectively.

Following its fragmentation in the 13th century, the territory was contested, ruled, and divided by a variety of powers, including Lithuania, Poland, the Ottoman Empire, Austria-Hungary, and Russia. A Cossack republic emerged and prospered during the 17th and 18th centuries, but its territory was eventually split between Poland and the Russian Empire, and later submerged fully into Russia. Two brief periods of independence

Figure A.21 Ukraine is a country in the CIS bordered by Russia to the east and northeast, Belarus to the northwest, Poland and Slovakia to the west, Hungary, Romania, and Moldova to the southwest, and the Black Sea and Sea of Azov to the south and southeast, respectively

Source: Worldtravels.com.

occurred during the 20th century, once near the end of World War I and another during World War II, but both occasions would ultimately see Ukraine's territories conquered and consolidated into a Soviet republic, a situation that persisted until 1991, when Ukraine gained its independence from the Soviet Union in the aftermath of its dissolution at the end of the Cold War.

Following independence, Ukraine declared itself a neutral state.[37] Nonetheless, the country formed a limited military partnership with the Russian Federation, other CIS countries and a partnership with NATO since 1994. In the 2000s, the government began leaning toward NATO, and the NATO-Ukraine Action Plan signed in 2002 set a deeper cooperation with the alliance. It was later agreed that the question of joining NATO should be answered by a national referendum at some point in the future.

Former President Viktor Yanukovych considered the current level of cooperation between Ukraine and NATO sufficient, and was against Ukraine joining NATO. In 2015, protests against the government of President Yanukovych broke out in downtown Kiev after the government made the decision to suspend the Ukraine-European Union Association Agreement and sought closer economic ties with Russia. This began a several-months-long wave of demonstrations and protests known as the Euromaidan, which later escalated into the 2014 Ukrainian revolution that ultimately resulted in the overthrowing of Yanukovych and the establishment of a new government. These events precipitated the Annexation of Crimea by the Russian Federation in February 2014, and the War in Donbass in March 2014; both are still ongoing as of December 2015. On January 1, 2016, Ukraine joined the Deep and Comprehensive Free Trade Area with the European Union.[38]

---

[37] Parliament of Ukraine 2007. "Declaration of State Sovereignty of Ukraine." Verkhovna Rada of Ukraine, https://weA.archive.org/web/20070927224650/ http://gska2.rada.gov.ua:7777/site/postanova_eng/Declaration_of_State_Sovereignty_of_Ukraine_rev1.htm, last accessed 01/28/2016.

[38] Balmforth, R. 2010. "Yanukovich vows to keep Ukraine out of NATO." http://reuter.com/article/us-ukraine-election-yanukovich-idUSTRE6062 P320100107, last accessed on 01/28/2016.

Ukraine has long been a global breadbasket because of its extensive, fertile farmlands, and it remains one of the world's largest grain exporters. The diversified economy of Ukraine includes a large heavy industry sector, particularly in aerospace and industrial equipment.

Ukraine is a unitary republic under a semipresidential system with separate powers: legislative, executive, and judicial branches. Its capital and largest city is Kiev. Ukraine maintains the second-largest military in Europe, after that of Russia, when reserves and paramilitary personnel are considered. The country is home to 45.4 million people (including Crimea), 77.8 percent of whom are Ukrainians by ethnicity, followed by a sizeable minority of Russians (17.3 percent) as well as Romanians/Moldovans, Belarusians, Crimean Tatars, and Hungarians. Ukrainian is the official language of Ukraine; its alphabet is Cyrillic. The dominant religion in the country is Eastern Orthodoxy, which has strongly influenced Ukrainian architecture, literature, and music.

Ukraine's GDP per capita PPP, as depicted in Figure A.22, was last recorded at $8,267.07 in 2014, when adjusted by PPP. The GDP per capita, in Ukraine, when adjusted by PPP is equivalent to 47 percent of the world's average. GDP per capita PPP in Ukraine averaged $6,996.86 from 1990 until 2014, reaching an all-time high of $10,490.37 in 1990 and a record low of $4,462.78 in 1998.

Ukraine posted zero economic growth over 2012 and 2015 because serious macroeconomic and structural weaknesses remain unaddressed.

UKRAINE GDP PER CAPTIA PPP

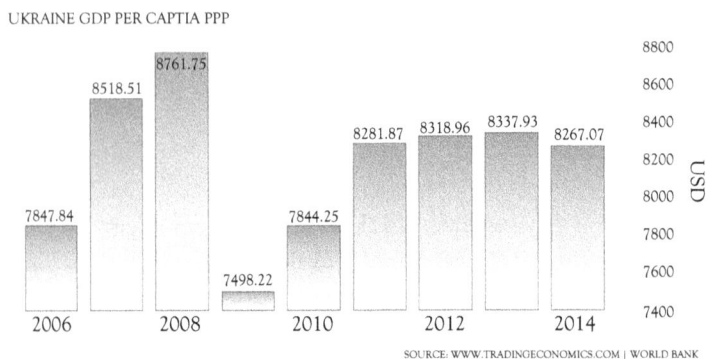

SOURCE: WWW.TRADINGECONOMICS.COM | WORLD BANK

Figure A.22 Ukraine GDP per capita PPP 2006–2015

Source: World Bank, tradingeconomics.com

A combination of de facto fixed exchange rate policy, loose fiscal policy together with considerable quasi fiscal subsidies in the energy sector has led to further widening of the budget and the external imbalances and threatens sustainability.

Top concerns for Ukraine now are the developments in the Euro zone and the state of the global economy together with resolution of the political crisis in the country. Confidence in the government and the state institutions is low. Economic growth remained weak for the last 2 years. After five consequent quotes of economic slowdown started in the second half of 2012, Ukraine's GDP posted growth of 3.7 percent y/y in 4Q2013 driven by good harvest and low statistical base. This brought FY GDP growth to 0.0 percent (after 0.2 percent in 2012). Performance of the key sectors remained week due to weak external conditions and delays in domestic policy adjustment.

Economic growth is expected to recover slightly in 2014, however the risks for this forecast are still substantial. On external side, the main risk is a protracted crisis in Europe, leading to lower demand for exports and more difficult access to global capital markets. Domestically, the main risk is a failure to implement macroeconomic rebalancing (preferably anchored in a program with the IMF). Delays in macroeconomic adjustment could mean that the forced adjustment will be much sharper. Ukraine's access to financing is already limited by investor concerns over the sustainability of its macro framework, political situation and the poor investment climate.

To support the banking industry, World Bank is actively working with the government and the National Bank of Ukraine and other financial regulators on strengthening the policy and regulatory role of the state in the financial sector, while consolidating state ownership of financial institutions.

Evidence shows Ukraine is facing a health crisis, and the country needs to make urgent and extensive measures to its health system to reverse the progressive deterioration of citizens' health. Crude adult death rates in Ukraine are higher than its immediate neighbors, Moldova and Belarus, and among the highest not only in Europe, but also in the world.

The unemployment rate increased to 9.5 percent at the beginning of 2009 because of the global financial crisis, and today stands at 7.5 percent.

While firms in the country face a shortage of skilled workers, many university graduates can't find employment or end up in jobs that do not use their skills due to skills mismatch.

Literacy and school enrollment rates are high in Ukraine. However, larger budget allocations to education have not resulted in improvements in the quality of education. Ukraine's priority should be to make better use of the resources allocated for the sector by significantly downsizing the school network to fit the smaller (current and projected) cohorts of students.

Ukraine has tremendous agricultural potential and could play a critical role in contributing to global food security. This potential has not been fully exploited due to depressed farm incomes and a lack of modernization within the sector. The establishment of a legal framework for secure land ownership, development of an efficient registration system, and ensuring free and transparent land markets are important elements of a policy framework that could facilitate agricultural development in Ukraine.

Ukraine is one of the most energy inefficient countries in the region and restructuring and upgrading its energy sector continues to be one of the key development challenges for the Government. The sector faces problems maintaining security, reliability, and quality of supply due to delays in energy sector reform, poor financial condition of energy sector enterprises, lack of investments, and deferred maintenance in aging infrastructure. These factors threaten the sustainability of economic growth, degrade the environment, and increase the cost of social services. Improving them is among Ukraine's top strategic priorities.

The municipal and services sector in Ukraine suffers from decades of underinvestment and poor maintenance. The need to invest in water and wastewater utilities is growing dramatically and the existing low tariff levels are a major limitation to the sustainability of utilities. The need for rehabilitation is exacerbated by the overall high-energy consumption in water production and wastewater treatment. Improving service delivery through rehabilitation of infrastructure and promotion of energy efficiency solutions offers the possibility of driving utilities toward financial sustainability while providing improved services.

Uzbekistan

Eastern Turkic-speaking nomads conquered once part of the Turkic Khaganate and later Timurid Empires, the region that today includes the Republic of Uzbekistan in the early 16th century. The area was gradually incorporated into the Russian Empire during the 19th century, and in 1924 what is now Uzbekistan became a bordered constituent republic of the Soviet Union, known as the Uzbek Soviet Socialist Republic (Uzbek SSR). Following the breakup of the Soviet Union, it declared independence as the Republic of Uzbekistan on August 31, 1991 (officially celebrated the following day).

Uzbekistan is a doubly landlocked country in Central Asia. It is a unitary, constitutional, presidential republic, comprising 12 provinces, one autonomous republic, and one capital city. As depicted in Figure A.23, Uzbekistan is bordered by Kazakhstan to the north, Tajikistan to the

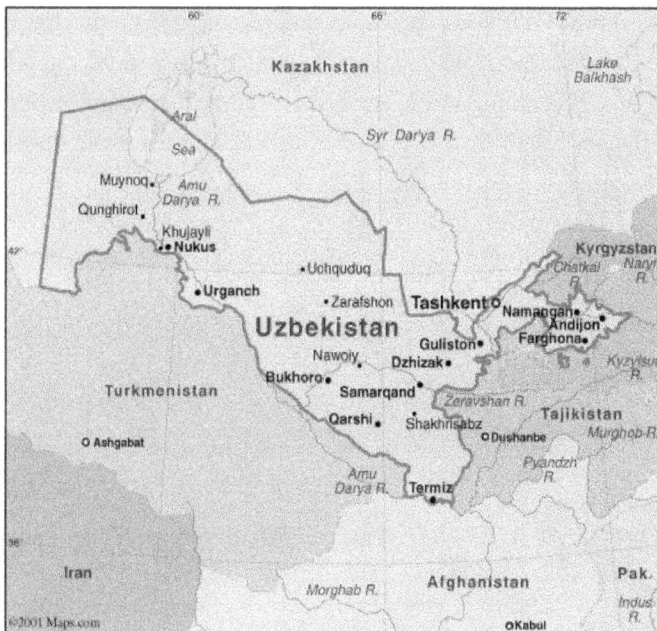

Figure A.23 Uzbekistan is bordered by Kazakhstan to the north, Tajikistan to the southeast, Kyrgyzstan to the northeast, Afghanistan to the south, and Turkmenistan to the southwest

Source: maps.com.

southeast, Kyrgyzstan to the northeast, Afghanistan to the south, and Turkmenistan to the southwest.

Uzbekistan is officially a democratic, secular, unitary, constitutional republic with a diverse cultural heritage. The country's official language is Uzbek, a Turkic language written in Latin alphabet and spoken natively by approximately 85 percent of the population; however, Russian remains in widespread use. Uzbeks constitute 81 percent of the population, followed by Russians (5.4 percent), Tajiks (4.0 percent), Kazakhs (3.0 percent), and others (6.5 percent). Most Uzbeks are nondenominational Muslims. Uzbekistan is a member of the CIS, OSCE, UN, and the SCO.

Uzbekistan's economy relies mainly on commodity production, including cotton, gold, uranium, and natural gas. Despite the declared objective of transition to a market economy, its government continues to maintain economic controls, which imports in favor of domestic "import substitution."

As depicted in Figure A.24, since the mid-2000s, Uzbekistan has enjoyed robust GDP growth, thanks to favorable trade terms for its key export commodities like copper, gold, natural gas, cotton, the government's macroeconomic management, and limited exposure to international financial markets that protected it from the economic downturn. Still, the future is not without challenges. The GDP per capita in Uzbekistan was last recorded at $5,319.50 in 2014, when adjusted by PPP. The GDP per capita, in Uzbekistan, when adjusted by PPP is equivalent to

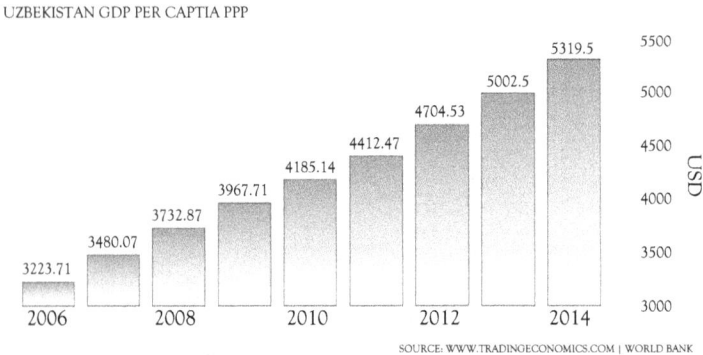

Figure A.24 Uzbekistan GDP per capita PPP 2008–2014

Source: World Bank, tradingeconomics.

30 percent of the world's average. GDP per capita PPP in Uzbekistan averaged $3,164.74 from 1990 until 2014, reaching an all-time high of $5,319.50 in 2014 and a record low of $2,216.68 in 1996.

Since the mid-2000s, Uzbekistan has enjoyed robust GDP growth due to its favorable trade terms for its key export commodities, the government's economic management, and limited exposure to international financial markets that protected it from the economic downturn.

Overall growth for Uzbekistan is projected to continue at around 7 to 8 percent annually during 2011 to 2014, supported by net exports and a large capital investment program. World prices for Uzbekistan's principal exports are projected to remain favorable at least through the first half of the 2012 to 2015 fiscal year Country Partnership Strategy period.

The impact of recent increases in global food and energy prices is expected to be limited given Uzbekistan's policy of self-sufficiency in both food grains and energy. Given the government's plans to finance up to two-thirds of their investment program from external sources, including loans, external debt is expected to increase gradually.

The country must contend with a combination of risk factors going forward, including deteriorating security conditions due to the situation in Afghanistan, and increasing tensions between its neighbors over regional issues, especially the management and use of transboundary energy and water resources. Domestically, Uzbekistan must work to minimize its economy's vulnerability to possible external shocks affecting commodity prices and the anticipated inflow of FDI and external loans to finance the large public investment program.

Uzbekistan, with the goal of becoming an industrialized, high middle-income country by around 2050, is continuing to transition to a more market-oriented economy to ensure equitable distribution of growth between regions and to maintain infrastructure and social services. The country's policy goals and priorities are: to increase the efficiency of infrastructure, especially of energy, transport, and irrigation; to enhance the competitiveness of specific industries, such as agroprocessing, petrochemicals, and textiles; to diversify the economy and thereby reduce its reliance on commodity exports; and to improve access to and the quality and outcomes of education, health and other social services.

About the Authors

Marcus Goncalves, EdD, PhD, is an international management consultant with more than 27 years of experience in the United States, Latin America, Europe, Middle East, and Asia. He holds a doctorate in Educational Leadership from Boston University. He has more than 45 books published in the United States, many translated into Portuguese, German, Chinese, Korean, Japanese, and Spanish. He's often invited to speak on international business, global trade, international management, and organizational development subjects worldwide. Marcus has been lecturing at Boston University and Brandeis University for the past 15 years. He has also been a visiting professor and graduate research adviser and examiner at Saint Joseph University, in Macao, China for the past 4 years. He is an Associate Professor of Management, and the International Business Program Chair at Nichols College, in Dudley, Massachusetts, United States. Dr. Goncalves can be contacted via e-mail at marcus.goncalves@nichols.edu or marcusg@mgcgusa.com.

Erika Cornelius Smith, PhD, researches and teaches the histories, politics, and economics of the United States, Central Europe, and The CIS as an assistant professor of history and political science at Nichols College. She holds a master's degree in political science from Eastern Illinois University, and a doctorate degree in history from Purdue University. Among many grants and awards, Erika held Title VIII Fellowship for Research and Training in The CIS and Eurasia, Indiana University and Russian and East European Institute. Dr. Smith can be contacted via e-mail at Erika.smith@nichols.edu.

Bibliography

Abdelal, R. 2001. *National Purpose in the World Economy: Post-Soviet States in Comparative Perspective.* Ithaca, NY: Cornell University Press.

Aceves, R. 2016, January 13. "Economic Snapshot for Central and The CIS." *Focus Economics.* Retrieved from http://focus-economics.com/regions/central-and-eastern-europe

Aghion, P., and O. Blanchard. 1994. "On the Speed of Transition in Central Europe." In *NBER Macroeconomics Annual,* eds. S. Fisher and J. Rotemberg, 283–320. Cambridge, MA: MIT Press.

Al Jazeera (2009). "Belarus shuns Moscow amid loan row." http://aljazeera.com/news/europe/2009/05/2009529121949669957.html, last accessed on 01/28/2015

Alam, A., P.A. Casero, F. Khan, and C. Udomsaph. 2008. *Unleashing Prosperity: Productivity Growth in The CIS and the Former Soviet Union.* Washington, DC: World Bank.

Andrej, K. 2015. "NATO2020: We need trust, solidarity, and resolve." *News release,* 11 November https://prezident.sk/en/article/prezident-na-nato2020-potrebujeme-doveru-solidaritu-a-rozhodnost/

Aristovnik, A. 2010. *The Determinants & Excessiveness of Current Account Deficits in The CIS and the Former Soviet Union.* Retrieved from http://wdi.umich.edu/files/publications/workingpapers/wp827.pdf

Armstrong, W., and J. Anderson. 2007. *Geopolitics of European Union Enlargement: The Fortress Empire.* New York: Routledge.

Åslund, A. 2001. "The Myth of Output Collapse after Communism." Carnegie Endowment.

Åslund, A. 2002. *Building Capitalism.* Cambridge: Cambridge University Press.

Åslund, A., P. Boone, S. Johnson, S. Fisher and B. Ickes. 1996. "How to Stabilise: Lessons from Post-Communist Countries." *Brookings Papers on Economic Activity* 1, pp. 217–313.

Axell, A. 2002. *Russia's Heroes, 1941–45,* 247. New York, NY: Carroll & Graf Publishers.

Balcerowicz, L. 1992. 800 Dni. Warsaw: BGW.

Balcerowicz, L. 1995. *Socialism, Capitalism, Transformation.* Budapest: Central European.

Balmforth, R. 2010. "Yanukovich vows to keep Ukraine out of NATO." http://reuters.com/article/us-ukraine-election-yanukovich-idUSTRE60 62P320100107 (accessed January 28, 2016).

Bandelji, N. 2007. "Supraterritoriality, Embeddedness, or Both? Foreign Direct Investment in Central and the CIS." In *Globalization: Perspectives from Central and the CIS,* ed. K. Fábián, 25–63. Amsterdam: Jai Press.

Barr, N. 2001. "Reforming Welfare States in Post-Communist Countries." In *Transition and Growth in Post-Communist Countries: The Ten-Year Experience,* ed. L. Orlowski, 169–218.

Barro, R. 1991. "Economic Growth in a Cross Section of Countries." *Quarterly Journal of economics* 106, no. 2, pp. 407–443.

Barro, R. 1997. Determinants of Economic Growth: A Cross-Country Empirical Study.

Beachain, D., V. Sheridan, and S. Stan. 2012. *Life in Post-communist The CIS After EU Membership: Happy Ever After?* New York: Routledge.

Blanchard, O. 1997. *The Economics of Post-Communist Transition.* Oxford: Clarendon Press.

Boycko, M., A. Shleifer, and R. Vishny. 1995. *Privatising Russia.* Cambridge, MA: MIT Press.

Calvo, G., and F. Coricelli. 1992. "Stagflationary Effects of Stabilisation Programmes in Reforming Socialist Countries: Enterprise-side and Household-side Factors." *World Bank Economic Review* 6, pp. 71–90.

Calvo, G., and F. Coricelli. 1993. "Output Collapse in The CIS: The Role of Credit." *IMF Staff Papers* 40, no. 1, pp. 32–52, Clarendon Press.

Cornell, S.E. 2010. Azerbaijan Since Independence. M.E. Sharpe. pp. 165, 284.

Dabrowski, M. 2015. "It is Not Just Russia: Current Crisis in the CIS." *Bruegel Policy Contribution,* 1. Retrieved from http://bruegel.org/wp-content/uploads/imported/publications/pc_2015_01_CIS_.pdf

David M. 2015. "Pro-Russian Estonia Mayor Arrested for Bribery." *Reuters,* 22 September http://reuters.com/article/us-estonia-arrest-idUSKCN0RM1R820150922

Dixon-Kennedy, M. 1998. *Encyclopedia of Russian & Slavic Myth and Legend.* Santa Barbara, CA: ABC-CLIO.

ETF (2011). *Labour Markets and Employability: Trends and Challenges in Armenia, Azerbaijan, Belarus, Georgia, Moldova and Ukraine.* Turin: European Training Foundation.

Feige, E. 1991. "Perestroika and Ruble Convertibility." *Cato Journal* 10, no. 3, pp. 631–653. Retrieved from http://object.cato.org/sites/cato.org/files/serials/files/cato-journal/1991/1/cj10n3-2.pdf

Filatotchev, I., M. Wright, and M. Bleaney. 1999. "Privatisation, Insider Control and Managerial Entrenchment in Russia." *Economics of Transition* 7, pp. 481–504.

Fox News 2006. "Turkmenistan's Leader Promises Citizens Free Gas, Electricity and Water Through 2030." http://foxnews.com/story/2006/10/25/turkmenistan-leader-promises-citizens-free-gas-electricity-and-water-through.html (accessed January 28, 2016).

Frankel, J.A. 2015. *Capital Flows to Emerging Markets*. Institute of International Finance. http://valuewalk.com/wp-content/uploads/2015/10/IIF_Capital_Flows_Report_10_15.pdf

Goncalves, M., J. Alves, C. Frota, H. Xia, and R.V. Arcot. 2014. *Advanced Economies and Emerging Markets: Prospects for Globalization*. Business Expert Press.

Heenan, P., and L. Monique, eds. 1999. *The CIS Handbook*. Chicago: Fitzroy Dearborn.

Hoogvelt, A. 1997. *Globalization and the Postcolonial World*. Basingstoke: Macmillan.

HRW 2014. "World Report 2014: Turkmenistan." https://hrw.org/world-report/2014/country-chapters/turkmenistan (accessed January 28, 2016).

Human Rights Watch, World Report 2015. Kazakhstan. https://hrw.org/world-report/2015/country-chapters/kazakhstan (accessed January 28, 2016).

IMF 2016. World Economic Outlook: Subdue Demand, Symptoms and Remedies, World Economic and Financial Surveys, Washington, October.

International Energy Agency 2012. "Oil Market Report." https://weA.archive.org/web/20120518015934/http://omrpublic.iea.org/omrarchive/18jan12sup.pdf (accessed January 28, 2016).

James, R., R. Atoyan, B. Joshi, and K. Krogulski. 2014. "25 Years of Transition: Post-Communist Europe and the IMF." *International Monetary Fund* (October 2014), p. 15.

Khanna, T., K.G. Palepu, and R. Bullock. 2010. *Winning in Emerging Markets: A Road Map for Strategy and Execution*. Harvard Business Press.

Kornai, J. 1992. *The Socialist System: The Political Economy of Communism*. Oxford: Oxford University Press.

Lange, O. 1936. "On the Economic Theory of Socialism: Part One." Review of Economic Lessons from Post-Communist Countries', Brookings Papers on Economic Activity, 1.

Mau, V. 1996. *The Political History of Economic Reform in Russia*, 1985–1994. London: Centre for Research into Communist Economics.

McKinnon, R. 1992. "Taxation, Money and Credit in a Liberalizing Socialist Economy." In *The Emergence of Market Economies in the CIS*, eds. C. Clague and G. Rausser, 109–28. Cambridge, MA: Blackwell.

McKinsey 1999. "Report on Russian Economic Performance." *McKinsey Global Institute*, www.mckinsey.com

Norman M.N. 1995. "The Russians in Germany: A History of the Soviet Zone of Occupation, 1945–1949." *Harvard University Press*, p. 70 Google Books.

Olcott, M.B., A. Anders, and G. Sherman. 1999. *Getting It Wrong: Regional Cooperation and the Commonwealth of Independent States.* Washington, DC: Carnegie Endowment for International Peace.

Parliament of Ukraine (2007). "Declaration of State Sovereignty of Ukraine." Verkhovna Rada of Ukraine, https://weA.archive.org/web/20070927224650/http://gska2.rada.gov.ua:7777/site/postanova_eng/Declaration_of_State_Sovereignty_of_Ukraine_rev1.htm (accessed January 28, 2016).

Peroti, E., and S. Gelfer. 2001. "Red Barons or Robber Barons? Governance and Investment in Russian Financial–Industrial Groups." *European Economic Review* 45, pp. 1601–17.

Press Service of the President of the Republic of Belarus 2004. "Section V: Local government and self-government." Constitution of Belarus, Archived from the original on December 17, 2007, https://we.archive.org/web/20071105204240/http://president.gov.by/en/press19333.html (accessed January 29, 2016).

Sakwa, R., and M. Webber. 1999. "The Commonwealth of Independent States, 1991–1998: Stagnation and Survival." *Europe-Asia Studies* 51, pp. 379–415.

Kundera, M., and G. Stokes. 1991. From Stalinism to Pluralism: A Documentary History of Eastern Europe Since 1945.

Taagepera, R. 1997. "Expansion and Contraction Patterns of Large Polities: Context for Russia." *International Studies Quarterly* 41, no. 3, pp. 475–504. doi:10.1111/0020-8833.00053

Tadeusz, S. 1995. *Russia and Azerbaijan: A Borderland in Transition.* New York, NY: Columbia University Press.

Temkin, G. 1989. "Economic Calculation under Socialism." *Communist Economies* 1, no.1, pp. 31–59.

Temkin, G. 1996. "Information and Motivation: Reflections on the Failure of the Socialist Economic System. *Communist and Post-Communist Studies* 29, no. 1, pp. 25–41.

World Bank 2015. "Doing Business: Georgia is this Year's Top Reformer." http://worldbank.org/en/country/georgia/overview (accessed January 28, 2016).

WTO 2012. "Accessions: Belarus." https://wto.org/English/thewto_e/acc_e/a1_belarus_e.htm (accessed January 28, 2016).

Zarakhovich, Y. 2006. "Kazakhstan Comes on Strong." *Time*, http://content.time.com/time/world/article/0,8599,1539999,00.html (accessed January 28, 2016).

Index

OTHER TITLES FROM THE ECONOMICS COLLECTION

Philip Romero, The University of Oregon and
Jeffrey Edwards, North Carolina A&T State University, Editors

- *A Primer on Macroeconomics, Second Edition: Elements and Principles, Volume I*
  by Thomas Beveridge
- *A Primer on Microeconomics, Second Edition: Competition and Constraints, Volume II*
  by Thomas Beveridge
- *International Economics, Second Edition: Understanding the Forces of Globalization for Managers* by Paul Torelli
- *A Primer on Microeconomics, Second Edition: Elements and Principles, Volume I*
  by Thomas Beveridge
- *A Primer on Macroeconomics, Second Edition: Policies and Perspectives, Volume II*
  by Thomas Beveridge
- *Basic Cost Benefit Analysis for Assessing Local Pubic Projects, Second Edition*
  by Barry P. Keating and Maryann O. Keating
- *Money and Banking: An Intermediate Market-Based Approach, Second Edition*
  by William D. Gerdes

Announcing the Business Expert Press Digital Library

Concise e-books business students need for classroom and research

This book can also be purchased in an e-book collection by your library as

- a one-time purchase,
- that is owned forever,
- allows for simultaneous readers,
- has no restrictions on printing, and
- can be downloaded as PDFs from within the library community.

Our digital library collections are a great solution to beat the rising cost of textbooks. E-books can be loaded into their course management systems or onto students' e-book readers.
The **Business Expert Press** digital libraries are very affordable, with no obligation to buy in future years. For more information, please visit **www.businessexpertpress.com/librarians**. To set up a trial in the United States, please email **sales@businessexpertpress.com**.

www.ingramcontent.com/pod-product-compliance
Lightning Source LLC
Chambersburg PA
CBHW050124210326
41519CB00015BA/4097